|||| Father ↑ Genocide ||||

MARGO TAMEZ

TURTLE POINT PRESS
BROOKLYN, NEW YORK

Copyright © 2021 by Margo Tamez

All rights reserved. No part of this book may be reproduced or transmitted in any form by any means, electronic or mechanical, including photocopying, recording, or any information storage and retrieval system, except as may be expressly permitted in writing from the publisher.

Requests for permissions to make copies of any part of the work should be sent to: Turtle Point Press, 208 Java Street, Fifth Floor, Brooklyn, NY, 11222
info@turtlepointpress.com

The author wishes to acknowledge the following publications, in which the following poems or portions of poems previously appeared in somewhat different form:

"Premont," from "Bird Boy of the Blue Light," *Raven Eye*, University of Arizona Press, 2007. "Kónlíjíh | to the river," from "To the River;" "Post | Memory," from "The Afterbirth Poem, (9)" *Hungry Spirits Rattle*, MFA Thesis, Arizona State University, 1997. "Rivered rememberer," from *Entre Guadalupe y Malinche: Tejanas in Literature and Art* edited by Inés Hernández-Avila and Norma Elia Cantú, The University of Texas Press, 2016. "Father replays the funeral in Dream #28," in poets.org, 2019.

Library of Congress Catalogue-in-Publication Data
Names: Tamez, Margo, author.
Title: Father | genocide / Margo Tamez.
Identifiers: LCCN 2021021125 | ISBN 9781933527048 (trade paperback)
Subjects: LCGFT: Poetry.
Classification: LCC PS3570.A446 F38 2021 | DDC 811/.54--dc23
LC record available at https://lccn.loc.gov/2021021125

Design by Phil Kovacevich

ISBN: 978-1-933527-04-8

Printed in the United States of America

First Edition

"The question of genocide is never far from discussions of settler colonialism. Land is life—or, at least, land is necessary for life."

—Patrick Wolfe[1]

CONTENTS

HERSTORY

19 Time bending in El Calaboz | The dungeon
21 Push
22 While counting steel posts, homeland is fracked, I embody penitentiary philosophies
23 How Lipans received the horse
24 Enemy Slayer teaches the first horse laws to Lipans

FATHER

27 Shika'ééhíí | Fractal memories   7018 Glendora
30 Cassette | October 15, 1996
31 Unburying his archive
32 Brecksville, Ohio
33 Waiting | journey
34 The waiting room is an archive
35 |||| Go sit down and wait until you're called ||||
36 Bendingtimeplace
37 Where did all the good men go?
38 Black men in the VA recognized your fractured | Indian | invisibility |
39 Black men could say the obvious
41 Cowbird receives an unexpected horse song
42 |||| Of |||| things |||| said |||| and |||| unsaid ||||
43 It's dangerous to type the issues you make me think about
44 Ruins as archive and lodges where knowledge sits
45 Of things in silence
46 Of archival silences and power exercised through archives
47 Horse carries the fourth arrow for Lipan woman

GOOD | MEN   Things that happen

51 Oral herstory
52 Creation story
54 Family reunion fragmented knowledge
55 Yamoria's laws
56 Oral tradition

WHEN WE WENT TO WAR

59 When we went to war
61 Peace treaty teachings by Shash Hastin Isdzán (Great Mother Bear)
62 Indian war herstory
63 Low-intensity conflict   ICC Docket 22
64 Prior Proceedings | Docket 22
65 Findings of Fact | Docket 22
66 Dad, you are on my genocide map
69 When a Lipan woman refuses extinction   she disrupts anthropological genocide

FLAVIA

73 Premont
74 1937
75 Outside water
76 My father's father, Premont, 1938

AMERICAN | FATHERLANDS

79 Zero sum: family history
80 Roosters
81 Ethnographic Tamaulipas
82 Kónlíjíh | to the river
83 Puehpi socobí
84 ~~kohntsaa Maria Zuazua Lipan Carrasco Tamez Hispanic nobody (zero some disposal trajectory)~~
85 Great-grandfather's ancestral knowledge transfer

86	Robert Kleberg orders a concentration camp, erasure
87	The wall is not the wall
88	Kleberg posits extra-legal martial law to address complexity and scale
89	Opportunity
90	Even the blood-soaked dirt	breathes a small breath

| HORSE

| 93 | Horse people |

FATHER | GENOCIDE

97	Maria von Blücher's Corpus Christi
99	Barbed wire
100	Concordances: re-thinking *Blood Meridian* as American genocide literary porn
101	Chertoff

POST | MEMORY

107	Post	memory
108	Rivered rememberer
109	Father	shell, stump fever dream
111	On the move bending time [Enemy Slayer]
112	A reluctant witness [Enemy Slayer]
113	Star people

TIME | BENDING

117	Message to my father who went to live with the End of the World People
118	You were a universe being born
119	Loss tightens her hands around my larynx
120	A lightning bolt I see up ahead
121	Dáyáada baa' ínjúúli	Native superstition
122	Hypocrites and the Monster Slayer

123 Baby graves   dágóyé'éé (it is difficult)
124 Dágóghé 'é (hard time)
125 Dá 'aandí 'aa   (it is up to you)
127 Do eighteen-foot gulag cement and steel walls   contain?
128 Post | survivor

WHAT'S COMING

131 Under the crease of sky
132 Bending | the word | with my father
133 Our memories met briefly inside a circle
134 At the entombment
135 My father stays earthbound
136 Night will color a dream real different
137 Dream #27   Gowá shimaa [my mother's house]
138 Father replays the funeral in Dream #28
139 My father's nickname tł'éna 'áí si'a | moonlight luna
140 What's coming
141 What's still coming
142 My father wants a ceremony because the funeral wasn't helpful
143 Dream: He re-emplaces to a gokal nadekleshen nigusdzaan

WALLED IN

147 Walled in by history, we stay alive, we remain, nonetheless

149 Notes
151 About the Author

To Luis Carrasco Tamez, Jr.
(January 5, 1935–October 16, 1996)

Because he had few arrows
he   knew
defenselessness.

Because they took his story
he   knew
exposure.

Because they took his land
he   knew
isolation.

Because they took his language
he   knew
distrust.

Because they erased his people
he   knew
refusal.

k'á

What kind of person
would be able and willing
to accept the call to forgive,
forget, or reconcile in the
given context (that is, under
the circumstances of
massive impunity and
escapist forgetfulness)?

—Thomas Brudhold and
　Valérie Rosoux[3]

|||| Father  Genocide ||||

HERSTORY

Where did all the good men go?
Where did they go?
　　　—Luis Carrasco Tamez
　　　　October 15, 1996

"Counting the steel posts from inside the gulag." (Margo Tamez, 2016)

Time bending in El Calaboz | The dungeon

                        I've been counting metal posts   a long time.

                        Starting in 2009. Only way I
                        can hold   memory   is   remember the # of posts

               is   counting by touch   is   tap count tap count

right-hand   fingers & palm
thrum   each post   I walk   one end
                             to another. Losing

focus   border cops   & drones   advance
detain   & I tap   my phone
app   records   their words   my detainment
        at the wall.

                        Maybe it was 'cuz   a mind   gets rough a
      hardened gut

                        Gut rust.   Steel dust.   fracked in skin.
                        Gets in.   Gut memory.   Gut knot.

                        Ten   years.

                        Americans   disclaim   this gulag. That this space
                        is   American gulag.   Labor labor labor labor labor.

                        21st c. American   fort: (impunity)
                        Steel.   Cement.   Dispossess.   (immunity)
                        Copy.   Cut.   Paste.

                        Re-forged   remains   re-purposed.
                                   Vietnam's sheds extracted.

                        Carceral innovation.   Invoiced and dispatched.
                        Mass shipment.   El Calaboz to Gaza.

Ndé[x] history	welded in	American genocide.	Fracking earthquakes.
Earth	loops memory	bends time	reclaims herself.
Throws	floods	pandemic drought	subsidence.

Solders.   Subverts.

Then.   Now.

This   kind   of   distortion   takes work.
Takes   your   labor.
Takes   a   certain   philosophy   to work
the   logic.

At his end, my dad   wondered.
Posed questions:

Where   did   all   the   good   men   go?

                        Where   did   they   go?

---

[x] The people; Plains Apache; Lipan; Dene

Push

                                                  I walk and count   penitentiary posts.

My penitentiary guess: 2, 956, 800   bollard   posts
in Kónítsa įįgokÍyąą.   Each one   a broken promise
broken words   broken family   broken clan   broken memory
broken history   broken land   broken spirit   broken heart.

```
|||||||||||    |||||||||||    |||||||||||    |||||||||||
     |||||||||||    |||||||||||    |||||||||||
|||||||||||    |||||||||||    |||||||||||    |||||||||||
     |||||||||||    |||||||||||    |||||||||||
|||||||||||    |||||||||||    |||||||||||    |||||||||||
     |||||||||||    |||||||||||    |||||||||||
|||||||||||    |||||||||||    |||||||||||    |||||||||||
     |||||||||||    |||||||||||    |||||||||||
|||||||||||    |||||||||||    |||||||||||    |||||||||||
     |||||||||||    |||||||||||    |||||||||||
|||||||||||    |||||||||||    |||||||||||    |||||||||||
     |||||||||||    |||||||||||    |||||||||||
```

There are   no walls   in places   conducive for
settler   security   economic   traffic   flows   to
   keep   settler   genocide   supremacy   flowing.

The wall   is not   the   wall.

While counting steel posts, homeland is fracked, I embody penitentiary philosophies

> I'm tellin' you the truth
> I hope I'm not being too cruel
> Since you ain't playing by the rules
> I'm 'bout to kick you off your stool
>
> —Erykah Badu
> "Penitentiary Philosophy"

I speak a name out loud   counting   each   post

Tribute:

Nazim Hikmet   Ken Saro-Wiwa

    Nawal El Saadawi   Trinh T. Minh-ha

Dareen Tartour   Ai

Augustina Zuazua   Flavia Carrasco

                                       Matiana Montalvo   Juanita Castro

Kesetta Castro   Andrea Cavazos

                                       Petra Gonzalez   José Emilio García

Lydia Esparza   Chavela García

                                       Teresa Leal   Eloisa García Tamez

counting posts   beats
penitentiary   math
dungeon   beats
carceral   math
post   beats

                      land-fracked
                    settler   thieves
                    racist   hate
                    cracked   remains
                    oil   spilled   rust
                    gut   rot   knot.

How Lipans received the horse

To learn the horse story   you gotta offer a gift. It's the law of storying.
                                I need a bridle and a bit. A beaded one.

                                To hear *this* story, one must offer a horse.
                                A black horse.   And a horsehair rope.

                                Roll a tobacco.   Get the good kind.
                                Don't be cheap.

To hear the story, one must offer something of value   to storyteller.
Our twenty-first century   price   is relinquishing   i.e. #landback.
If your intentions are good   I'll grant   your request.

                                The protocol must be followed. Take it or
                                leave it.

Protector, Enemy Slayer, made the law.
If you want to *be* anti-racist, to *decolonize* your ways
                                you must follow Lipan isdzané* laws,
                                Protector's laws. That's poetics of protocol.
                                Story is truth.

            Protector, the   Enemy Slayer   isn't   gendered
male.   Stop reading   Apache   anthropology.
Smudge that   off.

How did Lipans receive the horse?   More than one way.
More than one place.   More than one time.

In the blue-stone time, this occurred for the Lipans in Big Water Country.

Long ago   Protector   knew about four ways,   four places   four times
when   horse   emerged.   Other protectors watched.
Enemy Slayer sang   songs   calling   four whirlwinds   from four points:
flank   under a shoulder   at both hips.   Horse's nostrils
*   moistened   breath   quickened.   Horse   stood up.*

---

* women

Enemy Slayer teaches the first horse laws to Lipans

Protector, Enemy Slayer, went to the stronghold place   you know this today
as the Guadalupe Mountains, over there.

Protector needed three more horses, so there could be four.   In the east, Protector found
the blue horse.   In the south, Protector found the white horse.   In the west
Protector found the yellow horse.   In the north, Protector found the black horse.

Protector called rain and wind   to surround the four horses.   Using sun's
blue light, Protector made a rope   lassoing blue horse.   The same way, Protector got
a white rope for the white horse.   With the light, Protector put a yellow rope around
yellow horse.   With the light, Protector   got the yellow horse.
        Protector sang for a black rope from sun's shadows at the end of the long day. With the black
rope, Protector guided the black horse.

They stood calmly as rain and wind subsided.   Protector sang for Cowbird, crow, and bat. Crow
received the black horse.   Bat boy received the yellow horse.   Cowbird took the white horse.
Protector, Enemy Slayer, took the blue horse.

The three helpers raced. Protector   instructed Cowbird to care for & guard three horses
        created laws for healing those who will get injured
                                when horse steps on a foot
                                when horse throws a rider
                                when horse bolts
                                when horse transmits spirit to a rider.

The healer who does medicine   to mend those riders
must mention our name in their prayer songs.

If they want   to be with that horse as a rider
they must first offer   a song in your name.

If they do anything   without first acknowledging your name   Cowbird
then horse can do whatever they want to the rider.

*Teach Lipans   to respect my laws,   I am the first child of Isanałesh**
I am the nephew of Shash Hastin Isdzán, Great Bear Mother,   lawgiver in kónítsaįįgokĺyąą,

Big Water Lipan country.

Know this.

---
* Dene Ndé ancestral holy being; transformer.

FATHER

shika'ééhíí my father

shik'ahgóní I have arrows

Shika'ééhíí | Fractal memories   7018 Glendora

#1

1968.   You cared for us when mom worked weekends.
You carefully tied our Keds shoe strings, not tight and not loose. You had us walk a bit, then re-checked to make sure.
You made the best Coney Islands, extra Longhorn cheese and onions, and ranch-style beans.
You barbequed hamburgers, chicken, and sausage at the same time. Just meat. No sides.
You took us to Stinky Falls, still a natural eddy, lush, not developed. You showed us the trail.
You taught us our connections to this Ndé water hole, oak-covered, shaded, and quiet.
You taught us not to disrespect kó   the water.   You gave us a grounded example.
You pointed to the White skinny dippers drinking and throwing their beer cans into the water.
You showed us   running   was vital.
You ran   miles   up and down I-35   told us   *watch me*   from the back porch.
I-35   cement strap   leashed Laredo to Duluth.   1, 568   miles   ninth longest   interstate   in the   US.

#2

In your lifetime, you probably ran that distance.

Sometimes trains
blocked us from seeing you. Freight
between us you, the highway. You wore a bright-orange jersey, adidas.

You went to Premont returned with Duke a German Shepherd.
A bush dog couldn't last cement heat. You found his trail when he ran away.

You had goals for our safety. In front of White folks, you laughed tensely kept
your head down avoided eye contact. I knew we weren't safe your
body tensed you acted weird you held my hand too tight blood drained
my fingers went numb.

You mowed the lawn of the Seventh Day Adventist Church end of the block. In
exchange, you made it a football field. You taught us how to receive
 your long

arrowed pass. How to tackle each other. Protection. I didn't know
you played football in Premont. I thought you just had a gift for running
 throwing and avoiding contact with them.

You took us to Breckenridge Park on Sundays. Taught us tennis, bought us rackets
& showed us rules. You watched tennis on T.V. It relaxed you.

You got angry when people over-cooked eggs. Triggered you. Using the belt on the
one who did it taught me there are cracks inside you rage
pushes through your fractured busted shell.

You took us to see *Jesus*
 Christ *Super Star* at the Broadway
 theater.
You got a piano and the sheet music. We got lessons.

What's the jive tell me what's happenin' *what's the jive tell me what's happenin'* *What's the jive*

tell me what's happenin'

what's the jive tell me what's happenin'.

#3

When fear imprisons the father   the whole family   internalizes   prison   through him.

As a Lipan man   in   S. Texas

traumacaged   what you became   without your mother.

Losing Flavia   was losing everything   to bond you   to   belonging.
Losing Flavia   was losing everything   to teach you   love   is not a strap.

Losing Flavia   was losing everything   to hold you up   not   strike you down.

Your   father   never   could   not
                 be   held liable   for a   Lipan   woman's
       death   by   body torment   death by   spirit   yoke

         in   occupied

         lands.

When   everything   collapsed   underneath us   you
you   went   home   to Premont.

You   returned   with   two   horses.

                    You   started   over.

29

Cassette | October 15, 1996

My father's dream for his family was the chance to belong.

To not fulfill that dream left a hole.

The soul wither fathers feel when they can't fix the hole
is a trauma.

If he can't protect his family what is left?

"Dad, 10/15/96" (Margo Tamez, 2018)

Unburying his archive

My father's last message
    recorded   24-year-old cassette

dated October 15, 1996, 6:00 p.m.
Brecksville, Ohio.

Buried in the back of a drawer in my desk
two decades, a traveler.
Ohio, Texas, Arizona, Washington, British Columbia, Alberta.

I commit to listen in 2018.   To sit with it; attend to it; to hear; to feel the tremors. On tape,
he's translating his parish priest's   sermon for the next week.
Themed: unconditional love.   Sitting in a government-issued   oak chair
Mom got   at a garage sale.

I hear and transcribe:
He's eaten supper. Just finished.
Washed his dishes. Tidied the kitchen with mom.
Settled down in his army-issued Gunlocke Tiger chair.
The old mudroom in a post-civil war era farmhouse.
His small office. He made do in the Chief's house.
He's gotta make do. He had to follow Mom.
She made it work. She was a nurse.
He, disabled. Him, unemployed.

Her, a "G" employee. Chief Nurse. Chief employed. Chief income.
Rural Ohio, a long way from Premont, Texas. Follows the Chief.
Chief Nurse US Veterans Administration.
One government post to the next. Texas, South Dakota, Puerto Rico, Ohio.

It was Wednesday.
Early morning.
After he dropped   her off   at the hospital.
He went to the   park reserve   to jog.   His routine.

On his way home, he stopped   at the   post office.
Picked up   the mail.

He returned to the government-issued   post-civil war   farmhouse
reserved for Chief Nurse.
He stumbled.   Letters and junk mail   tumble to the couch.

Brecksville, Ohio

The weather in Brecksville was in transition.
He was wearing a light jacket. The seasonal
change of weather, variations in daily
high and low temperatures, required layers.

Mid-October temperature ranges
freezing to sixty-one degrees Fahrenheit.

One must be prepared
for all weather types.
Sun to fog.
Downpours to flurries.

Fall foliage
peaks at this pivot
this turn, this shift.

He had advanced cardiac arrest.
He drove himself to the VA.
Merely one hundred yards from his front porch.

    If he imagined he was running
        to score an impossible
        touchdown he could arrive,
        he could score.

When he reached the emergency room
he was Chief Nurse's spouse.

    they didn't know
    He was a brown man
    in a jogging suit.

They told him to go sit down.
Wait to be called.

    He followed their orders.
    He obeyed.

Followed the rules.
Did what he was told.

    Complied.

Waiting | journey

Waiting
he collapsed into failure.

Chief Nurse   in Cleveland.
Meeting with a Black nurse   who would join her

as a whistle blower   a major case   in Cleveland, Ohio
against VA hospital   corruption   violations

of veteran's rights.

Chief Nurse would not   know
of his death   until hours later   that day.

His last   Dene Ndé migration   Earth to blue sky, to stars
was   October 16

1996.

The waiting room is an archive   [being cause and effect]

The cassette holds a   night-before-his-death   record.
His archive of duty, his archive of inner dialogue, his emerging questions daring

to turn his mind, his thought, his inquiry
at the archive   at hidden   time and memory.
To bend toward insight   buried   and retrievable.

Between recording one's beingness   and   being denied beingness.
Being unseen.

Between   what language and sound are   for the father
and what
words and sound and years   become in imagination.

What is included   what is excluded   are not the pressing concern.
Years dissolving my   obsession   with negative and positive space.

Now more   an under-developed   archive.

Alterations, lacunas, eliminations, hush.   Our unrecognized muzzled
co-existence.

Some stories are just   not told.   They're subverted.   Heard elsewhere.
In other time-space. They're left.   Folded inside and inbetween.   Not there. Not here.

This tape.   Twenty years after.   You're stilled. Your still.   You're still the
Other
|||| IN |||| DI |||| AN ||||

You waited in the waiting room   the waiting room   is an archive.
Brown and Black bodies

holding breath.

Holding our breath archives.

hushed hushed hushed hushed be quiet be quiet be quiet wait wait wait wait be quiet be quiet waith

|||| Go sit down and wait until you're called ||||

hush |||| behave |||| follow instructions ||||
be quiet |||| go sit down |||| wait your turn ||||
be good |||| follow the rules |||| wait 'til your name is called ||||

If stripping and illegalizing Lipan-Comanche inter-marital kinship language   was the first wall

the waiting room
is where we are conditioned
to practice disciplined
submission   to penitentiary soul strip.

Fragments of our being
being macerated

into slivers flecks scales chips bits patches blisters pocks

Bendingtimeplace

Where did all the good men go?

Where did they go?

      Force
removal
      extraction
encoding
      shame
ruled
      domination
servitude
      duty
time

                slayed   re-made

            them   men.

Black men in the VA recognized your fractured | Indian | invisibility |

In your oral tradition   you   shared   a story
that Black brothers   in your   hospital ward   said   they
saw you.

              Your   dimmed
                                           life history   *listen up*
and denied
I can see you

South Texas   Premont   Alice Kingsville   Falfurrias   sledge-hammered
them   Ndn   men.

Church and School   and vital records   lost   key
details   locating   the Indian   life   history

              in   South Texas.   They   those ones
              perceived   absence   in   relation   to
              being   broken   by   Whites
when   Indian boys   lost   permission   to know   themselves
inside   Natural   History   structured   as   primitive
         pre-history   Indian   boys   learn
         early   due   to   authoritative   museum   exhibits   of
         Primitive Texas Indians   insisting   the   correct   answer
         is
no   body   who actually is Lipan-Comanche   in South   Texas
can   be   Indian   in   Texas.

Black men could say the obvious

They could say the obvious to him with kindness.

Their oral history of us in South Texas came about because Black men learned what their grandmothers remembered.

Black men could say the obvious to a Lipan man, disposed by Texas, knowing Texas the way that Black grandfathers storied Lipans and Lipans storied Black presence both interwoven in a long memory of Texas.

Lipan and Black spectrum of being
                              in non-being

is a mode of being   neither the cowboy   nor the Indian
                            transgressing   binary   codes.   Like
prisons   Texans   took   Lipan's   for granted.

They couldn't   imagine life   without history dungeons   for Blacks and Natives
                                the thirteenth for Blacks   non-recognition for Lipans.

The Black man   could see him,   knowing   the recognized
                take dungeons   for granted   a Lipan self-limiting belief as
a frame
                of knowing.   Because the disposed   feel
                the White man's   furthest   extreme of   denial.   That
underlying   history   is a   permanent   resident.

They   understood   his masks   were loss   his fear   was loss of trust.
                                                Seeing   his life
as   he couldn't   speak   or think it
beyond   waiting   beyond running   beyond   numbing.

Where American   historical imaginary,
poetry and performance   limit   the evocation of difficult history,
intergenerational memory,   when there is   a "dire problem
of non-responsiveness
in the archives"   to the marginal or
"indigenous" epistemologies,"   [t]he marginal voices
do not conform [and]
do not adopt
the "powerful   western   frame of reference"
of the   dominant group,   [they] are ignored.

—Rodney G.S. Carter, "Of Things Said and Unsaid:
  Power, Archival Silences, and Power in Silence"[4]

Cowbird receives an unexpected horse song

> Say, man, I just don't understand
> What's going on across this land
> Ah, what's happening, brother?
> —Marvin Gaye, "What's Happening Brother?"

In 1973, Luna and Chief Nurse being far from Kónítsaịịgokĺyąą
in the city knew no healers in the city and got bucked from the horse
named working-class-low-income-racialized bodies blues

Motown and Black community came with songs.

Luna and Chief Nurse call for a feast. Call for a house blessing.
In the Catholic Ndn way. Luna and Chief Nurse re-make oral tradition

having read the news on their mia/pow bracelets they welcomed new healing songs
to mend the hurt of isolation.

Away from home, Luna remembers belonging when visiting Inupiaq elders when Airforce
stationed him in
Alaska.

1959, Yukon-Alaska border,
and again in 1972, praying

1972, with the Black community Elders, Mrs. James
and Father Ira Lott, when we lived in San Antonio
during the US war in Vietnam

|||| Of |||| things |||| said |||| and |||| unsaid ||||

> Silence implies voice.
> It does not equal muteness [...],
> simply the absence of sound,
> speech, text, or other sign. Silence
>
> said and unsaid
>
> can be actively   entered into,
> or, as occurs   where the power
> is exerted   over an individual or group,
>
> it is enacted upon that individual or group.
> —Rodney Carter

Audio on TDK D-60 (1996 tech) is better than I expected.

Luna knew the internal war escalated.
Luna knew they could build a wall   while they told brown and Black folx
to sit down and wait   in the waiting room
to wait our turn
to hold our breath.

Luna   you wore down the beads of your rosary
waiting to be seen   recognized.

I delinked from penitentiary silence.

Forged a new shovel to exhume our dead.

Our_Lady_of_Law&QuestionsOnLandReturn_draftinprogress.docx

Dispossession_by_Controversial_Suppression@silencedbystatestructure.genocide.com

Your DNA   maps a '96 terror-form   terroir-form.   Weaponized lands.
Whip-peon-ized landz.

It's dangerous to type the issues you make me think about

                                                            or words
I'm thinking about   into Facebook.

|||| Los Zetas, Inc. |||| Matamoros |||| Los Fresnos |||| Brooks County clandestine mass burials |||| rape houses |||| trafficking |||| despair|||| our dead and dismembered |||| 1915 Cameron County |||| 1916 Cameron County |||| 1919 Cameron County|||| the Lipans who remained |||| Premont|||| Kingsvillle|||| Alice|||| Raymondville|||| Jim Wells County |||| Willacy County |||| Kleberg Country |||| Falfurrias |||| Victoria |||| and so on.

We've hammered   Google juice   like shots   to build up   digital fortitude.
We don't want digital sobriety   on this next   little journey to the land.

A decade   dug in   we're plugged in
we're   the lightning cord

                                      we've jacklegged   a toolshed
                                      we're gearheads   exhuming

bitter storms   bitter lands.

I'm composed in your ledger your ledge   your now   your know ledge.

I'm positioned   in ruins   as archive. We are   arc and hive |||| ruins.
    We are   the earth lodge   memory   truthing   what happened.

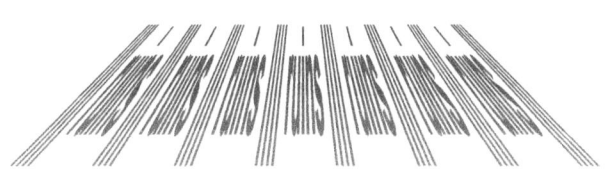

Ruins as archive and lodges where knowledge sits

Of things in silence

"The powerful have the ability to make lasting
statements that will be heard and attended to.

                                                                 Their words have authority and the power of the law
to back them up. Dissenting views, those of the marginal,

those statements that challenge or attempt to undermine
those in authority, are suppressed by the powerful.

                                                                 They are gagged, threatened, or otherwise
forcibly silenced. This type of silencing

has been called 'simple and perfect,'
where the individual or group is denied

                                                                 the ability to speak, to make a statement,
to voice their opinions."[5]

Rodney Carter, *Of Things Said and Unsaid*

Power *in Silence.* *Power* *Archival* *Silences* *and*

https://archivaria.ca/index.php/archivaria/article/viewFile/12541/13687

"Those who dissent are denied the ability to operate

within the discourse, what Lyotard terms the language

games. They are silenced through force [...]"

[Ibid. i.e., ditto]

Horse carries the fourth arrow for Lipan women

Protector traveled to the above world   in the blue line above the clouds.
There was a different horse   made there.   Made of star foam.
Protector used this for lungs.   Protector gathered hailstones floating in spirals
to make a liver.   A pair of bat wings   spread wind inside the lung
whirling air   to four places   on each flank.   Hail created teeth. Lightning charged pink
fleshy nostrils.   Evening star made eyes, providing night and day vision.
Ears formed from crescent moon   and rain made her mane and tail.

Milky way splashed down   creating her as roan, gray-white steel.
Enemy Slayer   protector of gray and white clouds   rider between Earth and Stars
placed corn stalk in the spine and legs. Her hooves given rainbow and rain. Under her hooves Protector Enemy
Slayer placed an invisible arrow.

Standing prepared, knowing   she'd return to Lipans as a woman
to bring the fourth arrow   and, to restore Lipan women

as law keepers.

GOOD | MEN Things that happen

        kó'shį'   somewhere
        kooka'yéé   where the camp is

        [even "where"   is implied as
                                  a water place
                                      in our territory]

Oral herstory

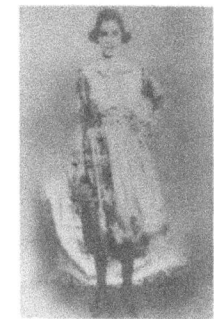

Flavia de la Fuente Muñiz Carrasco (Jumano-Lipan Apache)
daughter of Victoriana de la Fuente Muñiz
granddaughter of San Juanita de la Fuente
[...]

Dene   'k' dialect talking peoples   emerged through   Kónitsąąíí   Big Water

        [currently still spoken in northern
        Saskatchewan and northern Alberta]

        [Mexico, Texas, and the US annihilate
        "k" dialect, coercing "k"-talking people to speak Spanish, then English]

        [state-forced separation of a People; state-forced suppression of language;
        state-sanctioned distortion of the past; state-structured dispossession]

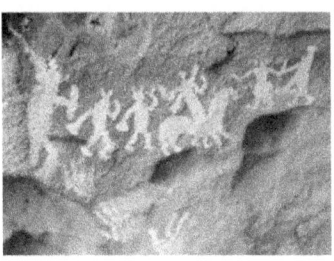

ha'shi 'dał'k'ida', 'áá'áná', 'doo maanaashni'   long ago   way back   remember

her ancestors traveled   nkaiyé   long walking people

dispersed by earth quaking   nkaiyé   long walking people

walking star birth water stories   nkaiyé   long walking people

painted belonging stories   nkaiyé   long walking people

Creation story

➤——→

Birth	infers death.
Death	supposes remembrance.
Remembrance	instils understanding.
Understanding	embeds a record.
A record	implies purpose.
Purpose	suggests reasons.
Reason	assumes intent.
Intent	denotes a plan.

Ussn* thought "be"

Ussn exhaled pollen	swirling	crystal black stone
Ussn exhaled pollen	swirling	crystal blue stone
Ussn exhaled pollen	swirling	crystal green stone
Ussn exhaled pollen	swirling	crystal red stone
Ussn exhaled pollen	swirling	crystal yellow stone
Ussn exhaled pollen	swirling	crystal white stone

You traveled space-time, a moon fractal, born January 1935 to Flavia.

Jim Wells County has no digital record of births in '35. Your siblings are recorded in 1926, 1928, 1930, 1932, and 1933.

In 1935   Woody Guthrie will write "So Long, It's Been Good To Know You."

In 1935,   the Texas White primary still exists, and it won't be struck down until 1944 by the US Supreme Court. Lynching of Blacks and Indigenous people is practiced in Texas, de facto.

The US Census does not count Lipans in Texas. By the time you are seventeen, a 12,000-year-old Indigenous burial site will be found in the Permian Basin.

---

* In Ndé creation story and oral history, Ussn is the name of the entity that created the universe and breathed life which created Earth, Moon, Sun, stars, and the outer realms.

1935, a major oil field is discovered in San Patricio County. The US Civilian Conservation Corps dispatch in Texas. In South Texas, anti-Black and anti-Indigenous racial incidents in CCC camps is high.

1935, through the CCC, Texas acquires Lipan homelands in the Chisos Mountains, Davis Mountains, and Mineral Wells into its state park system.

1935, estimates note the loss of topsoil was sixty-five tons per acre where settlers introduced planting corn in row formation up and down natural slopes. The soil kept washing away.

You were a toddler when Flavia died.

1937, her vital record notes she died of cervical cancer.

She was seven months pregnant.

She was thirty-two.

Jim Wells County had no treatment.

Indigenous women in Texas' lower Rio Grande Valley are twice as likely to die of cervical cancer compared to the rest of the US.

There are synergies between dysplasia
abuse   sexual oppression   isolation, colonization & cervical cancer.

At the family reunion, your father is a taboo topic.   Avoidance is a pattern.
Clan orature   dims him.

Family reunion fragmented knowledge

At a private reunion I arranged				in 2007
Flavia's surviving elderly sisters				said you cried inconsolably
								after she died.

You were still nursing.

Vital record:						You traveled space-time, a moon fractal
								born January 1935 to Flavia, Jim Wells
								County.

Your siblings and your aunties
								raised you.

								You would become an Oblate Catholic altar boy
and	#17 star	running	back				for Premont High.

								You ran away many times,		on foot.

Across Jim Wells, Brooks, Hidalgo, and Cameron counties.	Ancestral grounds re-scripted
to commemorate			mytho-history.

You graduated. Baylor offered you a football scholarship.	Your alcoholic father forbade it.
								Enlisted you in the airforce to support him.

The airforce stationed you					in Dene Yukon territory.

You married a Lipan-Peneteka woman				confronting colonizers
policing							ancestral territory.

You, the muted, molting and mutated

Luna		the aunties	called you	*the moon.*

Moon boy.
Moon boy.
Moon boy.
Moon boy.

		You arrived in a bitter land.
		You sang through your journey.	Music was your medicine.

Yamoria's laws[6]

Before modern Native Americans, Spaniards, and Anglos called us Lipans and Apaches we had strong relations in Denendeh–our ancestor place in the north.   Our language our perspectives originated there.

We have no words in our language for Lipan or Apache.   We have łbáí. We have Ndé.
That's a different story.   Survivors have other priorities.
Forgiveness   isn't appropriate.
Our homeland is Kónítsaịịgokĺyąą.   Big   Water   Country.

Yamoria   an Elder to   Enemy Slayer, Protector   is a transformer Timebender.   Yamoria made our   laws   lasting   deep time.

Colonization time   violated   Yamoria's laws. For future   reference.
Elders need to tell stories of the past, every day.   Don't sugar coat it.
Talk about good people. Talk about bad people.
Talk about mistakes people made.   Talk about the suffering this caused and to whom.
Try to prevent the mistakes in the future.   Work together.
Share everything you have.
Choose strong leaders with strong character, mind, spirit, and intelligence.
Women have rights to know everything going on   to decide how to eradicate injustice.
Parents need to share everything, take care of the sick, and help out in the community.
When people pass on, help the survivors.   Love each other.
Don't make others angry by your words or deeds.   Be respectful to everyone, especially strangers.
Be careful who you speak to.   There are people all around with bad medicine who will
use your words against you.   Bad medicine is being used all the time. Be aware.
Live softly on earth.   Have a good system to live softly on earth.
Communicate with each other well and often.   Communicate with love and soft hearts, even
when there are difficult issues to resolve.   Parents and families need to communicate about
planning for the future with Mother Earth.   Pray with the drum.
Feed the fire in honor of the spirit world.   Respect the spirit powers who protect Mother
Earth and watch from above realm.   Create ceremonies to honor the spirit protectors
from above.   Stop any wicked ways and stay focused on these
laws.   Remember to teach these and talk about these with the children every day.

Oral tradition

"Every Catholic diocese in Texas published Thursday the names of clergy accused of sexual abuse against minors going back as far as the 1940s."[7]

"Running away from home has often been viewed as one of the sequelae to sexual abuse."[8]

Genuflecting   faces dimmed   wilting   over the pew
numbed   penitents   converted   runaways

apostatada/os   runaways   euphemisms   rooted   in colonial control

whatever
feast day it happens to be.

Children's legs   held like plow handles.   To be plowed.

Texas roadside story-telling   normal   lies
traditional

              Great men's   plowing   history.

Runaways   needing to tell   who told
got re-told   as   "heathens," "liars," "illiterate."

Your hidden archives   called you home,

where Yamoria   threw down the lightning.

WHEN WE WENT TO WAR

When we went to war

Nobody wanted to hear   what   you   thought.   To the point
Texas   immersed   you   in roadside   genocide   history.

To attend school   was redundant.   A   killing history   epistolary
    planted   at   regular   intervals   anticipated
    you   panting   sweating   anxious   when   you ran
    down Texas highways   to escape   despair   in an open-air   cage.

When we went to war

we sheltered   children   women   elders   knowledge keepers

we shielded   Kónítsaįįgokíyąą

                                                belonging to us.

                                                          When we went to war

we guarded

we asserted   Kónítsaįįgokíyąą   laws

belonging to us.

                                          When we went to war

we informed   them   to follow   house   rules

we insisted   on   respect.   Matriarchal   laws

belonging to us.

When we went to war   we   knew   they   refused
culpability.

They   de-linked   us   from a   post-1870s   future.

They wrote   us   "dead"   predicting   our   illness
                as   measured   economic growth,

conditioned on   bodily   and mental   harm,
        structured on   bodies of the group,   inflicted   as
        measures of control   isolating the group,

calculated to bring   physical   destruction   individual   and collective
organized   depletion,   intended   to decrease,

        to diminish,   to   prevent births within   the group,   forcibly
        separating   children   from   ideas   theories   memory   of
the group,   to   sever life-affirming knowing sung by   mothers   grandmothers

        to sons   and grandsons,   to rupture   collective trust   between
        extended family   group members,   such   as   relative
        Indigenous   peoples   kinship   ties   we stitched to make us whole
        deciding   who and what   adoption   needs to be   amongst survivors.

Nobody wondered or asked   you   what you   thought
how   you   had   theories   on   Ndé
who remained   who didn't die   who didn't leave   who put on masks.

Nobody allowed   any questions   which   challenged
roadside   history   natura*lies*ing   genocide.

Land-locked within
KingKlebergKenedyCameronHidalgoStarrWebbJimWellsHoggBrooksSanPatricio

you   force   swallowed   normal lies   a curriculum & religion

mental steri*lie*sation.   Premont   &   Kingsville   ripped

Ndé   rainbow   paint   off   your   memory.   You
had no   protection.   No   protection.

60

Peace treaty teachings by Shash Hastin Isdzán (Great Mother Bear)

Endangering Ndé treaties of peace with Shash Hastin isdzán and Ndé grandmothers structured the wars without end. After the second Dene migration Ndé Kónítsaįįgokĺyąą peoples walked down branches of massive mother oak across Nigusdzán
    clan branches flowing Great Bear Lake water nourishing new beginnings.

Ndé Kónítsaįįgokĺyąą peoples matured in roles learning protocols given by Dene lawgivers we carried to our places.

Ancestors, Isanałesh, and Protector Enemy Slayer made the first treaty with Shash Hastin isdzán, Great Mother Bear. A loving contest ensued to prove to the Matriarch of Kónítsaįįgokĺyąą
    that Dene followed Her laws to live in synchrony with all sentient beings.

When our ancestral matriarch Shash Hastin isdzán observed our ancestors making sacrifices and learning consequences for violating Her trust & accountability
    she jumped into sky & rumbling thunder & lightning descending she pounded her fist into earth with magnitude.

Causing waters in four directions to flow into lands that she gifted to the Dene Ndé. Her gift would be their forever home place where they arrive after the earth shakes. Now, water would be balanced for the Dene Ndé. Ensuring Dene nkaiyé long

walking ways, ensured connection and futurism.

In Great Bear Lake where Isanałesh and Enemy Slayer emerged, the Matriarch ensured continuity and peace in Kónítsaįįgokĺyąą.

Indian war herstory

When George W. Bush claimed "there ain't no Indians in Texas"

he meant Texans' founding claim to exclusive title to Ndé lands cleaved & obscured Ndé place via shoving Indians

inside Texas history.

This meant

                    J. Bourke   M. Gamio   T. Kate
A.F. Bandelier J   J. Moody   J. Walter Fewkes

the constabulary facilitating
settlers sustaining place vis-à-vis
dodgy narratives.

broken   **broken**   **broken**   **broken**   **broken**
    broken   **broken**

broken   **broken**   **broken**   **broken**   **broken**
    broken   **broken**

Low-intensity conflict   ICC Docket 22

In 2007 a law professor at U. New Mexico advised:

"Don't ever forget this crucial fact. The Spanish military and, later, the US department of war adopted and then re-invented the term 'Apache.' It's a weapon."

They needed to mass produce an idea to win the Indian War for industry and banks. After all do you know of any

Indigenous peoples who would refer to themselves as "enemy" as their everyday identity? You know to actively disown

their Indigenous identity in unceded lands and instead to claim a Eurocentric term: "Apaches" which is in law of conquest a

     legal term that works against their own best
     interests as Aboriginal peoples in their homelands?

Thousands of Ndé in Texas barely survived
     low intensity conflict war.

"And, know this, a principal case for Aboriginal title throughout the western legal system is ICC Docket 22, Lipan v. U.S. 1971. UT Law doesn't teach this, as you intuited."

Prior Proceedings | Docket 22

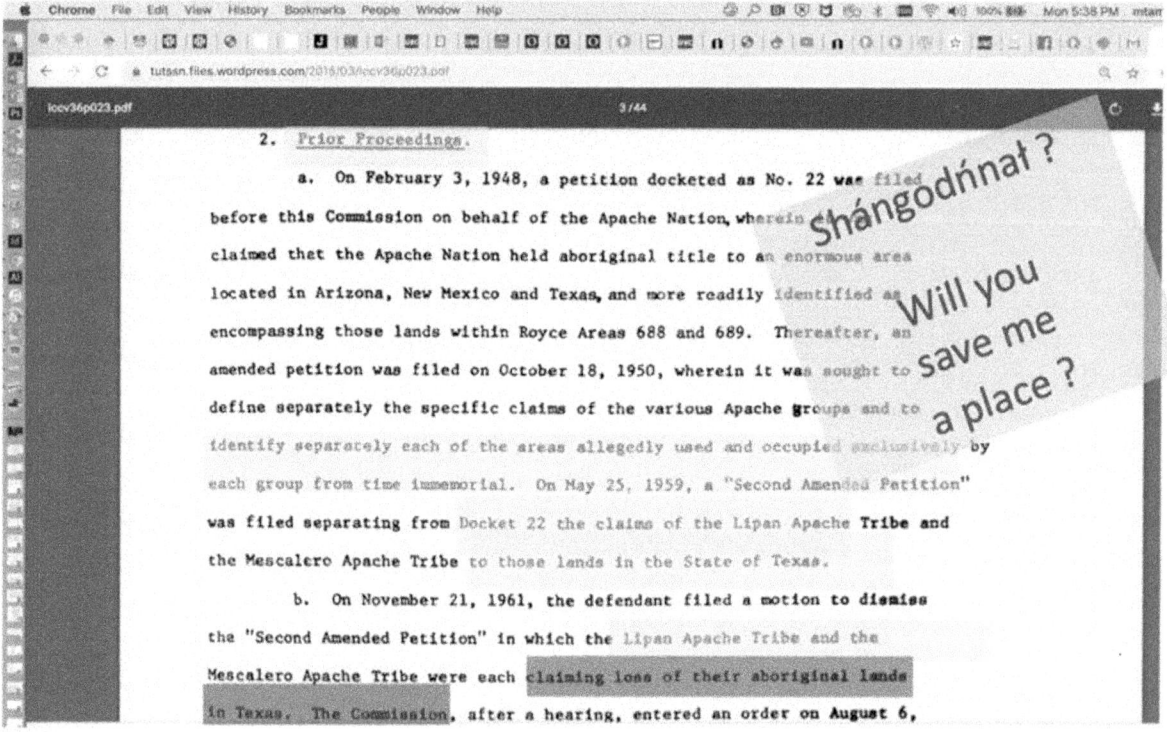

Findings of Fact | Docket 22

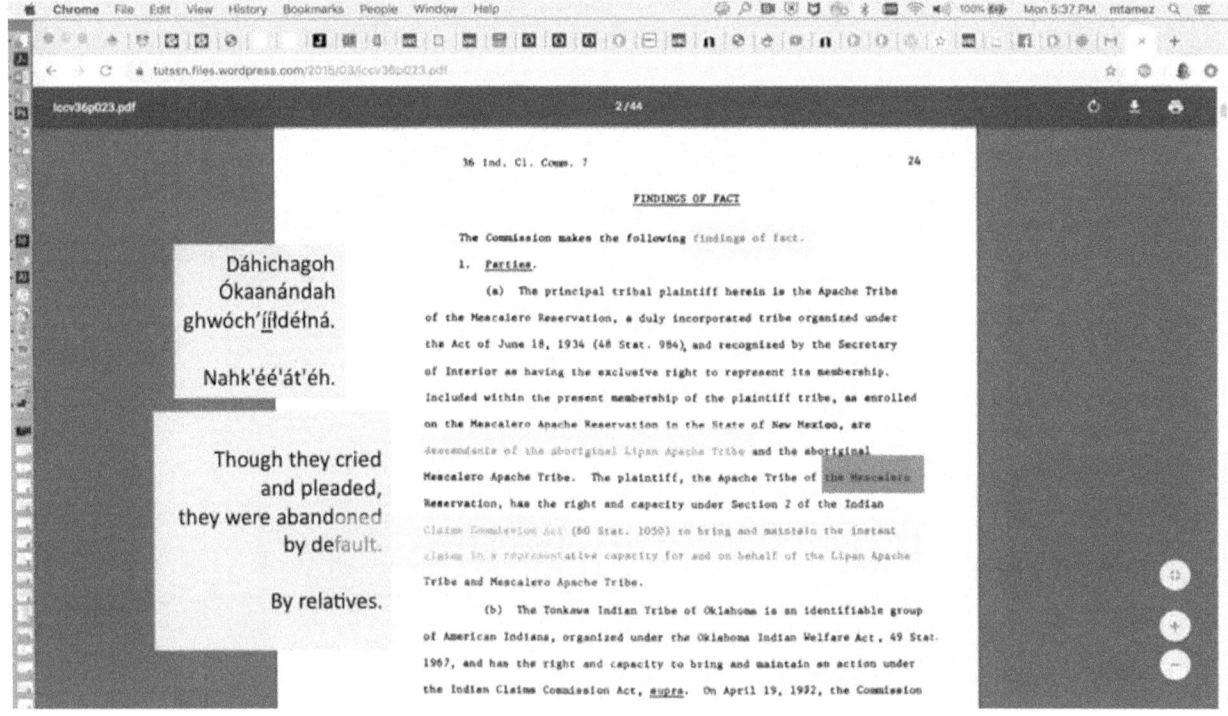

Dáhichagoh
Ókaanándah
ghwóch'íį́déłná.

Nahk'éé'át'éh.

Though they cried
and pleaded,
they were abandoned
by default.

By relatives.

Dad, you are on my genocide map

> War with the American settlers also reflected competing visions of land use in Texas that would shape its subsequent history.
> —Ben Kiernan[9]

I know you had no real access to address the
cognitive neurological, emotional, mental,
and physical challenges you experienced
your entire life. I recognize the dehumanization
you experienced in the many institutions and
systems you navigated, and which ultimately failed you.

You died before I could share some sources to
help you find answers to your questions. The
questions you planted sprout and re-germinate
perennially, offering new linkages between
violent victimization that Flavia and relative
Indigenous women in S. Texas experienced
throughout their lives.

These sources, while disturbing and potentially
triggering, reconfirm and affirm family stories,
collective memory, and the oral history of
settler colonial violence damaging each tree
branch in our community-wide forest, over decades.
I wanted to share these before you died.
I didn't get that chance.

You, in our expansive blue spirit world,
I offer these up to you, and hope these
help you find peace everlasting, and
will heal those parts of you broken, as
you are part of the generation, raised
by those who survived the nineteenth century.
I now understand this happened to us,
and is still ongoing.

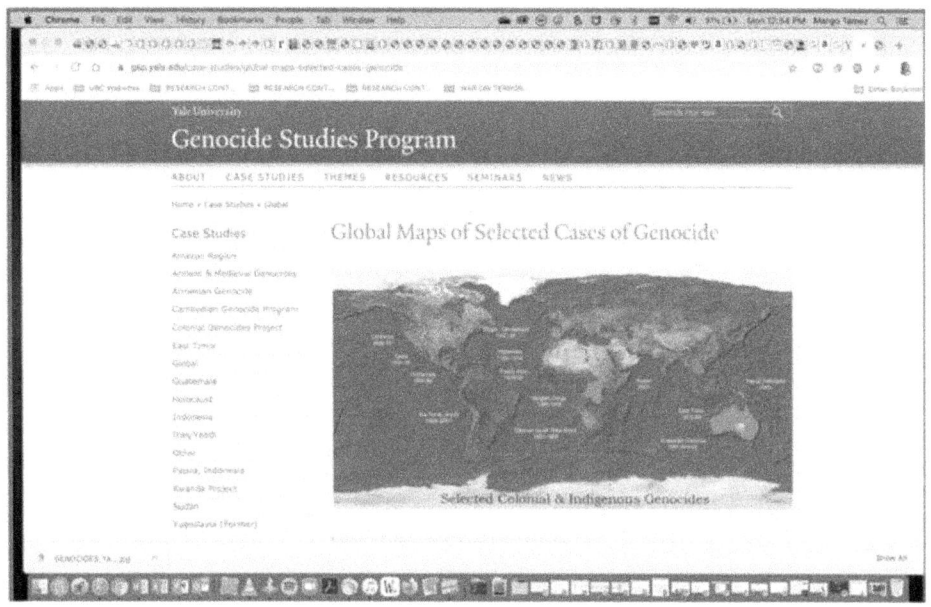

Extermination is a process, which includes, though is not always at all times about the destruction of bodies.　　　　Ideas　are like　　　holsters　　　　　for guns　　　　like　　the train bringing soldiers　　　　　the Spencer　　　　for militias　　　　a household budget　　upholding White women's　　　supply and demand　 of her munitions　　　　　to disaggregate　　　Ndé mother's　　　place.

Requires　*certain bodies*　　　*embodying*　　　ideas　economies　　civic duty　polities　　　　identities united　　　　　　under certain conditions　　 land　 blood　　　　religion familybirthright　　　　　　　culture language　　　　　superior entitlement.

Specialists　　unique people　　　　　　seeking willing eager serving　　　　exceling　　　innovating　　collaborating　cooperating　　occupying　　　developing.

Dad　　　　when you grew up　　　in Premont　 &　　Kingsville
settlers no longer called themselves settlers.　　They called themselves *Natives*.
They called themselves *heroes*.　　　　They called themselves *pioneering*.
They invented everything.　　　　They patented history.　Synonymous
with taking.　　Leaving us the shatter zones.　　Shredded.

This made existence feel like fog.　　Cognitively rejecting Lipans' survivance
in their plain sight　　　　was synonymous　　with faking　 genocide didn't happen.
En masse gas-lighting.

67

Dad, another thing.　　White settler women's place on the land　　　　couldn't thrive
without White settler men　　claiming Nativeness.　　　　White women made worlds, too.

This is where White women　　obfuscated Lipan women　　still living.　　Ordered
and filed away, under *removal*.　　　This happened as a process. In time, we
thought it was normal　　　to be marching　　　at school.　　In single file.　Ordered.
Following orders.

You won't find the footnote. This is
the *hidden* part
of active　　　celebrated　　　suppression.

68

When a Lipan woman refuses extinction she disrupts anthropological genocide

> At the time this account was recorded, there were very few Lipan;   today there are no Lipan speakers; hence the Lipan are,   like so many other Indian tribes,   wholly extinct.
> —Henry Hoijer[10]

Beware   when   anthropologists   use   "ed"   past tense   to describe their   interviewee's   community   as "moribund"   *while* they   interview   *her*.

American ethnographers   witnessed   &   surveilled   Ndé   being   starved   as a   weapon   to force   Ndé   to cede   surrender   leave or die.

American linguists   arriving later   witnessed   only captured Ndé   on   a reservation.

Based on   a small sample   three   reported back to the government reservation Ndé in New Mexico   "living"   uncaptured majority in Texas: "extinct."

According to Jumano Apache oral tradition, in Redford   Big   Bend   they witnessed soldiers in Mexico   marching   captured   nineteen Lipans   from Chihuahua   handed them   over   to U.S. soldiers   in   La Junta. Marched them to New Mexico.   Prisoners   included   women and children.   Case closed.

Dáxà'dą   kónìcąą   'ìsjáánìí   yààgòòłnìì
'áí   màagòčàlnìnìí   'áyídìí   bìkì'ìsčíí
'ákò'àà   'áí   kónìcąą   'ìćísjáánìí   màagòčìłnìì   'áǰìníínìí

Long ago   a Lipan   old woman   she told about it.
   That   *that* she told about   *that*   I am writing it.
   And then   that Lipan   old woman   she told about it
   in   that   which   she spoke.

In oral   spoken   and   written   Augustina Zuazua   former prisoner of war

told   Harry Hoijer   Lipans   still remained.

In the late 1930s   as a Ndé war survivor, she   shared   her   biographical story   establishing   Ndé   homelands   stay   alive   in   oral   tradition.

War doesn't separate Ndé   from   belonging.   In 310 sentences   she recorded   place names   encompassing Texas   New Mexico   Chihuahua   Coahuila   Big Bend   Lower Rio Grande   homelands.
Augustina   talked   back.

FLAVIA

        ndi'níí   your mother
        yénáałniná   she remembered

dáá'ko'aah nádiidzáná isdzáníhíí   then the women arose

Premont[11]

> Flavia, your mother, is pregnant, has cervical cancer, you are nursing, Premont, 1937.

We exist as light from a gas lantern
mantles wilting like sacs of skin. Your fingers
search soft nails pinch all I have left. Your delicate nails.
You've learned about clutching each moment before absence.

Your rooting mouth rejects my nipple, fever hot, giving way to mastitis
blocking milk ducts.

You are kó water
glowing under a frail bridge
      collapsing like loam.

We are two mountains beyond the wasteland
through cold.

The foreground shimmers that's you. I am: amaranth and flow.
Beyond: the blue light.

No matter you remain.
A part of self in another's life. For you to see.

Remember to listen.
  Feel birds singing today.

1937

| Flavia, pregnant seven months |
fetus | your father immobilized

I am water without moisture.   Numbing day
                    my hand   cut   arcs
liquid   furrow.   Growing
ribbons veining   facia   weights
submerged.

Your body's   sex   one   long   bleed
a narrow slit   incision   I'm a door
jamb   and hallway.

Your body is a story   jammed.
White man's
story eclipsing yours   hauling away   chipped   debris,

your father's   your son's   an axed   oak.
Memory is a chasm.   A glacial crevasse.

Old story.   Your story   stalls out.

Don't   silently watch me   wash   my vagina's discharge.   Don't accuse me
      of witchcraft   infidelity   being   shameful.

The metal is   sharp   cold   and I   need   more hot water.   Please observe.
Be present.

Watch my skin grow air
                    bubbles attaching to blood draining.

My body sees but prefers
memory   body's story   fizzling

frayed cuticles
blue veins   flesh   cells   scabbing

a ropy terrain   scarred   extractions.   You want sex.

Flesh holding flesh   a body's attack

retains   belonging.

Outside water

I
Flavia thinks of the man she needed him to be

You lean toward the body outside water

"rise up."

You want to see folds of skin   from births
this scar   above my brow   points to sky
fine hairs at   the navel forming   passage to my womb.

I hear doves through a crack
crumbling ceiling

sound like sprays of water,
their fine wings moving,
like sounds of your breath   submerged
in the past, separate, apart

where you acknowledge
we're not   recognized
no standard history.

You are   a re-becoming   human.
You are enough   to hold   the living and the dead.

| My father's father, Premont, 1938

Unyielding wind   scorch-eyed
you take Flavia's sister
to raise your clutch of nine

        you   micro-burst
going off   on shenanigans   your bets   lost the land
you are hail   dinging and gouging
    you're unbuckled   a gun unholstered   your bit is bloody the bridle hard and cracked.

You are glass fragments   scarcely attached   to caulk
a door busted and piled into scraps.

Hail marking small o's   floodland floodplain plain
o's and wind

mojave bad medicine made this   "fuck-up" song
mojave bad medicine berated   "son-of-a-bitch"   gallivant gallivant gallivant

you bent the sky to fractals
    her holograph mirage   can't-bring-you-back songs
  your antiquity,
    o in your mind

the o disbelieve
the o doubt
the o fear

your efforts expunge
your spleen.
There you are   spit   and   hammered
recognizing truer truths
you   won't   *ever repeat*.

AMERICAN | FATHERLANDS

To unmask what should stay hidden,
To "develop" the negative.
—Ai, "Finnegan Awake," *no surrender*

Zero sum: family history

"Texas stands third among the states, after Mississippi and Georgia, in the total number of lynching victims. Of the 468 victims in Texas between 1885 and 1942, 339 were black, 77 white, 53 Hispanic, and 1 Indian."[11]

"The difficulty I had in recognizing [...] the Indian [...] is rooted in an ideology that denies the presence of Native Americans in the north of Mexico—including those provinces of colonial Mexico now known by the name (sic) "Texas" [...]."
—David Frye[12]

As in removing from the land equation. Take 'em out. As in
private property is done on a body. Bodies on bodies.

To get a zero-sum result they zero some out.

There aren't accountancies
no concordances
no statistical studies
nor comprehensive models examining S. Texas'

                                          lynchings
                                          live burnings
                                          killing fields
                                          clearances
                                          massacres
                                          slaughters
                                          blood baths
                                          assassinations
                                          dismemberments
                                          mutilations
                                          indignities to dead bodies
                                          scalpings
                                          grave robberies of

Lipan Tonkawa Karankawa Jumano Comanche Coahuiltec peoples' lands.

Indians as vanished is zero-sum zero some profit.

Roosters

> As the narrative embeds Texas Mexicans deeper and deeper into the historical fabric of South Texas, peoples and things [I]ndigenous to the region slowly fade away. This erasure of "the Indian" serves two functions: to disrupt totalizing Anglo appropriations of history and modernity on one hand, and to substantiate the claims to history, place, and contemporary citizen-subjectivity the text makes for Texas Mexicans on the other.
> —Kirby Brown[13]

```
Extend their necks      then a quick twist and      a snap.
The heads                           twitch a bit    side to side.


Buttery hued beaks              arched crests      feathers        quelled
juvenile                        necks              jagged as first teeth   like jawbones of seagulls
on a tarred shore               bones              tendons                 taut.


Sometimes they'd     wash up
                                to river banks      Nueces, Frio, Trinity   I also saw them
at the Rio Grande by Redford           heard about more       at the Pecos       and piled
along                           the lower Rio Grande.

Rivers          relocate        wash                secrete.


Grit            gravel          silt        soil        sludge
river           reeds           clog        shore       scrape
collect         gurgle          stems       clash       mud.


My father               taught                          snap    the necks
                        just so.
```

Ethnographic Tamaulipas

        Tam ho lipam

        (Place where the Lipan pray/prey, [Huastecan])

Tamaulipas: Situated in the extreme northeast of Mexico
                                       in the Huasteco region seamed together with Texas | U.S.
                                       Rio Grande river.

        Huastecos are Mayan descendants,
        speak (téenek)   historically
        shared   region   with Nahua

        shared   region   with   Apachean and Comanche peoples.

(Enciclopedia De Mexico, Torno XIII, Arizona State University library,
stacks reference material.)

        Lipan Apache: A Dene-Ndé Peoples
        diverse ways and many clans,
        communities, whose migrations emplaced them
        in a long-memory, long-history relationship
        with lands bifurcated by the
        Canadian-US and US-Mexico
        settler colonial borders.

(Oral tradition.   Suppressed in unpublished journal notes. Linguists specializing in Na-Dene.)

Kónlíjíh | to the river

You walked alongside Grandpa   passed the storage hut
  his boundary tree marked with Great-grandpa's knife. You'd just
  returned   USAF tour Alaska.

  Tilted planks windows boarded. He showed you where Great-
grandma did his ceremony   cleaned him up WW2 dimmed his shine.

She removed a shadow   eating his lungs.
  He   thought   you needed this story.

After he died they bulldozed her place
    removed her weavings.

He gave you ha 'ich'idéé*

     keep   ha 'ich'idéé dánzhó'é**

 she told him.

Past a chain-link gate past Falcon Dam
go up river   to those   Red Paint people, your canyon cousins.

Follow the river.
Keep away   when you see

American men. Their

    metal over the land

make your earth-mud mash with the medicine
in your palm.

Trail away from them.
Press this medicine all over yourself. Sends ghost sickness away.

---

* Bear root; osha
** Respectfully; in a good way

Puehpi socobí*

                Blood   land

                (a) limping home   (a homeland paved over, suffocating)

caane yocoró

                                        Comanche Street, Drive, Avenue, Loop, Trail, Park, Lookout, Road, Depot, Lake, Springs, Creek, County, Library; Edinburg, TX; Corpus Christi, TX; Laredo, TX; Beeville, TX; San Antonio, TX; Uvalde, TX; Camp Wood, TX; Comanche, TX; Kempner, TX; Austin, TX; San Marcos, TX; New Braunfels, TX; Fredericksburg, TX; El Paso, TX; Presidio, TX; Lajitas, TX; Ft. Stockton, TX; Katy, TX

fire   moon
ember   flicker
fuse   dim   blister smolder   raze

                                            lodged   dislodged

caane yocoró   limping   lodge

homeland   char   singe
                                             ashes   sear

limping

---

* Peneteka Comanche dialect, El Calaboz, Lower Rio Grande Valley.

~~Kohntsaa Maria Zuazua Lipan Carrasco Tamez Hispanic nobody (zero some disposal trajectory)~~

| Lipan Street @ Artesian Street, Corpus Christi, Texas

hummingbird
hands   washing

sway-backed   she wrings
slings into   a dollar-tree basket

wet sheets   hang-dried

nettles   idling   the intersection
flanked   fringe

spur   barb
punchy

unseen   obscure
veiled   shadow
unnoticed   unseen

many   ~~Marias~~

no   last   name

redundant   surplus

homogeneous   same   pavement   illegible

| Great-grandfather's ancestral
knowledge transfer
Jim Wells County, 1915

> The Apaches of Arizona, as well as the Indians of the Territory
> shall be given every guaranty; and their lands which have
> been taken from them shall be returned to them,
> to the end that they may assist us in the cause which
> we defend.
>   —*Article 5,* Plan de San Diego,
>   Rio Grande Valley, South Texas, 1915

Making deals to retake what was already yours   under another's cause
reduced   our future.

Rifles stood upright   leaning with tips angled

toward a   crease of two walls

faint moon ray;   you thought

if we are not already dead   we must resist that they think
we may as well be.

Night was dark   sight was worse than hearing.

Staying alive   reduced nonetheless   the only thing left.

                 Kédaadidliiná. They prayed.

| Robert Kleberg orders a concentration camp,
erasure, Cameron County
Late November, 1915

[read: "ethnic" ~~indigenous~~ and ~~inter-racial indigenous~~ peoples ~~not sequestered into U.S. Indian reservations in Texas~~ and 4~~th class~~ citizen-laborers in the Texas-Mexico ~~stolen lands belonging to Lipan Apache, Comanche, Nahuatl-Tlaxcaltecan, Carrizo, Coahuiltecan Indigenous communities~~ in the Lower Rio Grande region engaged in ~~armed resistance~~ struggles. Indian War. ~~On-going.~~
~~Falls off the register of normative American Indian and Native Studies scholarship or Genocide Studies~~.]

Mexicanizing   Lipan Apaches   into "ethnic Mexicans" normalized/s
genocide
second wave.   It's an innovation in hate speech.

Winter 1915, Cameron County.

Annihilation   gets scripted   as

orderly efficient   proper
                disposability;   requires vetted proposals

            contracts   good economy

            measurable outcomes
            remote [sequestered]

extra-legal [unregulated by law]   historical distance.

            Reiterated   killing is
            legal.   Modernity's rhetoric   masks   how Lipan-Comanches
            are   dissolved   discursively   in/as   social death.

Killing   is
                    fungible | unregulated by law.

            Kleberg   architects
            martial law   along the river

        | unruled bodies being
        | the dead   not dead; hidden in plain sight/site.

86

The wall
is not
the wall

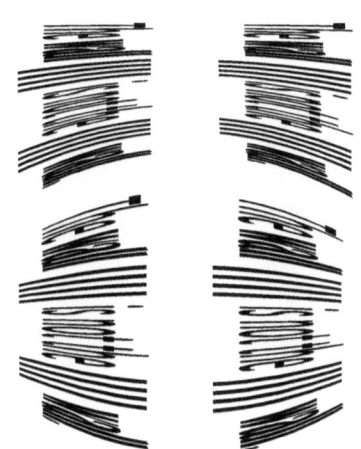

| Kleberg posits extra-legal
martial law to address complexity
and scale

[subtext: multi-indigenous resistance to organized, industrialized
martial force substantially increased in local guerrilla metrics]

        Kleberg   like his German father   insisted
        progressive   accountancy
        elicits | productive results.

        Those unaccounted for   would be   hypothetical
        internment [collected] | detained   in the   camps

        by the river | could be   reinforced   in El Calaboz | the dungeon.

        Mexicans call that place   El Calabozo | hold them   the undisciplined
        in a 100-mile swatch | inland.

        Gain   operational   control.

| Opportunity   Lower Rio Grande
river edge, near La Encantada
[the enchanted], 1916

Employ camp inmates
clear carrizo cane along river's edge
        and inland
deploy 110,000 military troops.

Coerce resisting Hispano-Tejano ranch owners.
Put 'em in there with indigenous dissidents.
Accuse them of colluding with the insurgents.

Get into   El Calaboz, El Ranchito   and La Encantada.
Invade capture   vanquish   subdue   all enemies
Reduce   reduce   reduce.
Get control.

Get the names   force names from insurgents at La Encantada.
Suppress   the rest.

Protect   settlers   established families.
Protect   investments.

Round up and shoot all who remain.

```
Even the blood-soaked dirt            | breathes a small breath


Feather noises              infant song
dangling                    somewhere near.


Even sound                  degenerates

                This time               all of us

huddle                          herd              underground.


You are                     seasons             swifter       bending

a moment        releasing

dianthus
                curving

silk line
                gums

lattice leaves
                mulberry

sigh-songs
                swift

clasping
                presence

push
                breath

morning
                fog.
```

HORSE

Today's Comanches are arguably descendants of an empire people, but we go unrecognized by those who leave their representations of us in the distant past or, just as problematically, view us as remnants of a once powerful people, as if we are more of Comanche heritage than we are real Comanches.
 —Dustin Tahmahkera[14]

Horse people

Some of us belong in spaces and kinships
complicating Americans' understandings of place,
nation, peoplehood, heritage, ancestry, national languages,
territory, family, family cemeteries, family history, law,
governance, and jurisdictions.

Horse is our kin.

There is no border	no fortress	no distance	no obstacle
too great	to ensure	one's	kin
will	thrive	and	expand.

Photo digital alteration (Margo Tamez, July 4, 2020)
Original photo: Wikipedia. Wild Horses of Placitas.jpg Created: 25 December 2012.

FATHER | GENOCIDE

Maria von Blücher's Corpus Christi: letters from the South Texas frontier, 1849–1879

"Red Indians" as rationale for aggression, violence, weaponizing settler fragility and impunity against accountability for destruction of "savage Indians"

"Red Indians" as normative backdrop upon which German settler population possess, accumulate, build economies premised upon Indigenous extermination, at the discursive, psychological, physical, material, spiritual, linguistic, and symbolic

"Our land on the Nueces" as description for presumption of German settler ownership of unceded and non-surrendered Indigenous homelands

"I have a Mexican washerwoman" as articulation of presumption of German entitlement to possession of the labor, bodies, and production of strongly suggesting poor, subjugated, oppressed, mixed-race Indigenous-Hispano women.

"I have a Mexican;" "our Mexican;" "my Mexican" repeated frequently throughout

"Indian corn" as articulation of the prevalence of the labor of Indigenous peoples, knowledge systems, generosity, and strategic planning against scarcity under violent colonization by both Hispano and northern European settlers, and the backdrop upon which German settlers enabled their survival on the backs of subjugated labor and feudal system ensuring their advancement

"Felix is still away measuring land for the German Emigration Association" as articulation of interlocking role German settlers played in illegal land surveying, recruitment, and settlement of German emigrants and immigrants in unceded and non-surrendered Indigenous territory

"black people;" "black woman;" "blacks" as articulation of a motivation to acquire Black labor in order to have "some pocket money" for iced lemonade, bullfights, and silverware, etc.

"Little Mexico;" extralegal killing of Mexicans seeing, witnessing, though not questioning or using her social status to challenge overt race-based violence and mass killing as a first-hand witness

"Corpus Christi" and "stores"	obsessive focus on the "advancing" order of a Eurocentric economy catering to a German sensibility and desires for "good umbrellas" amidst en masse killings occurring against "Red Indians,", "Mexicans," and "Blacks"
"Send me some things"	certain German settler occupation, land possession, development, survival, and prosperity in S. Texas and LRGV occurred with regularized & reliable economic support from their parents, kinship, pointing to the German elites' class investment in taking, dominating, securing the colonization vis-à-vis dispossession of Indigenous peoples, and labor and resource extraction. This triangulation is a structure and root in the making of Texas.
This is the interlockingness	of things, economies, bodies, White settler women's belonging
and possessiveness,	of their naming of the order of things, bodies, justifications
for	violent dispossession.
Never	naming the process and the erasure
	genocide.

Barbed wire

> Capitalist concentration itself, rather than the produce of the Great Plains, would be the true economic significance of barbed wire. The promise of the Great Plains gave a push to an industry of a certain tools of violence, and this industry gave a push to the concentration of capital.
> —Reviel Netz[15]

In Texas, wealth disparity between Indigenous peoples and Whites is viciously observed along barbed wire fence.

Barbed wire puts in stark relief physical separation economic stratification social degradation spiritual desolation of Indigenous peoples forcibly removed from land water sacred sites and sites of memory.

Wealthy classes monopolize resources and accumulation through aggressive policies enacted physically through barbed wire.

Whole communities surrounded by barbed wire, creating Indigenous ghettos in remote, rural, and urban areas.

The compulsion to fence out Indigenous rights underscores the built world of open-air prison and detention architecture normalized throughout Texas.

By 1900, Texas leads the continent in bringing space under control to bring cattle to market, to expand mass markets, and to gain operational control at significant scale. Barbed wire enabled an upscaled colonialism intensifying the technological bandwidth settlers weaponized on a global level.

By 1915, gaining operational control over Lipan, Comanche, and relative lands became an obsession.

Became necropower.

"Americans embraced the violence of barbed wire, just as they embraced the violence of competition to which it gave rise."[16]

Concordances: re-thinking *Blood Meridian* as American genocide literary porn

Terms	# of mentions
Men	254 (men not Indigenous)
Blood	147
Dead	139
Naked	91
Bones	75
Kill	55
Savages	47
War	41
The black	41 (as racial reference)
Apaches	40
Coins	40
Women	38 (women not Indigenous)
Gold	34
Gun	24
Silver	23
Murder	19 (non-Indigenous characters are "murder"-able)
Texas	16
N-word	16
Humans	4 (not referencing Indigenous or Black bodies)
Dead squaw	1

Chertoff

1.
You were born November 28, 1953.
According to the Chinese zodiac, you arrived under the sign of the snake.

"Wish You Were Here" shut down at the Imperial Theater
Alabama beat Auburn 10-7, Birmingham
Hamilton Tiger-Cats defeated the Winnipeg Blue Bombers, 12-6.
On the surface, there was order.

Though 1953 was a pivot for re-arranging the planet's DNA, sparks vaccine testing,
Truman announces American hydrogen bomb development R&D,
Crick and Watson pierce the double-helix polymer,
Salk starts polio clinical trials,
Hillary and Norgay claw to the summit of Mount Everest,
Queen Elizabeth II dutifully performs conquest rituals in Westminster Abbey,
Fidel Castro sparks anti-imperialist dissent in Cuba,
Bantu Education Act establishes the legal scaffold for apartheid,
The UK initiates surveillance on citizens to track their use of TVs,
KTSM TV, channel 9, El Paso, broadcasts for the first time,
East Germany ousts corrupt elites from government,
the US telecasts its first transmission to Canada,
Waco is overturned by a tornado.

2.
Trauma in America will be transferred between generations.
Older generations pipeline their trauma to future generations.

Desensitization between
older generations transfers desensitization to next generations.

America desensitizes to violence.
There are no laws in most US states
legally requiring anyone
to learn Indigenous history.

3.
Studies show Holocaust survivors pass trauma on to their generations.
Some refer to this as an *inheritance of terror*. Much is written on this.

They say that one-third of Americans deny the Holocaust.
In some places, denying the Holocaust is dangerous, illegal speech.

4.
Most Americans deny the Indigenous-American genocide.
This denial is not illegal in the United States, nor anywhere else on our planet.

5.
In your future, I am offering testimony in tribunals about your role in the wall.
I am forcing a national conversation about the relationality between American genocide,
Texas, what we can learn from Jewish Holocaust survivorship experiences in the US,
on-going denial of Indigenous genocide, and Indigenous historical genocide erasure
in the US.

In your future, I will tell the world I am concerned that you
are the author and architect
of the 2006 Secure Fence Act, and the Section 102 "mega waiver,"
which criminalized Indigenous women's resistance against US dispossession and
state sanctioned terror.

6.
I ask, what happened between Elizabeth, New Jersey, 1953 and El Calaboz, Texas 2006?

What were the gaps in your education and teachings?

Why do you not see   that we are Indigenous   and   are   here?

7.
As a public servant, who did you serve most   least? Where did you learn
it is okay   to deny   Indigenous   are human, too?

8.
According to teachings, those born under a Snake sign are goal-focused,
will even hide in Horse's hoof to cross the finish line; to the detriment of Horse.

9.

|||| your Wall

zero-

summing ||||

																											transgenerational trauma																											
																							makes you								a real																							
							American man															

POST | MEMORY

You say you want this story
in my own words,
but you won't tell it my way.
—Ai, "Interview with a Policeman," *Fate*

Post | memory   October 1996

You say look to the blue
                          red will send me to a nucleus
                          pinhole of pallid light

turn left at the tunnel
an opening door   marked   blue disk

shades one   injury   at a time   then you'll see
a rise   hill

one locality   one geography   time.   Look for unused coals
the ash pile   keep them

water woman's prayers sit there
a cross-hatched mesquite stack   ready for the lit match.

Uninterrupted soundlessness   erasure   glows
off-the-record   unofficial   discreet   evidence

continued existence.

Pass this forward.

From there   pray with wild-rose water
for remembrance

                               spin and spool this, then
weave language

                               color and fibers

a heaping spectrum.

Rivered rememberer

When I was a girl   the river wasn't a border.
At the shoulder   my grandparents waited
just until we were out of sight.   They'd slowly
step out of ánáashdlééhja 'át'é*   skins

revealing river snakes   embodied.

They'd return to the river
wait 'til we fell asleep   lips of our eyes parted   the whites in
five children enlacing   first and second cousins   around the one-room shack.

Enclaved in El Calaboz | (the dungeon)
handfuls of wild clover   stuffing them into our mouths
                    bloating stomachs | dim-lit lamp posts

filled with green saliva | Military Highway/281   striated   forensic archaeology
an equation of looped history
                    repeating pattern around remains
boarded-up windows
leaning plank walls.
                    Aging aunts and uncles living
                    on that side of the Big Water**
a serpentine ribbon   saying something about our small place

not big enough   not a town   two perpetual halves
                    far-gone divisions   more | less.

Going off the lines   meant arriving   musky heat   Aunt Chavela's kitchen.
Tamale-love threshold.   Earth cookies. Military Highway 281 | masking resistance
barbed   containment   feast   days
knotting   river peoples'
spatial sound   sculptures   English-Spanish-Nahuatl-Comanche-Apache.

Fibrous language painters   they had to, not thinking why.
More than watermarks   edges of official memory
ledgers distorting   blood-treks   blood-traces
a complicated kinship | as blood-lines go.

---

* Human, Jicarilla-Apache-English.

** Kónitsąąíígokíyaa, Big Water People's Country [homeland].

Father | shell, stump fever dream | October 1996, Brecksville, Ohio

My father lies still   remembering someone's love.
Whose love   was the   [_____]   he tried to fill.

His gray hair matted   into a sweaty cotton sheet
   telling me: war is marked in witchcraft

buried in the ground   metal nails   beads.   Our own Stockholm Syndrome.
Pitched cicada   leg-rubbing   "this is the end" chorus

shedding skin   a kind of cleansing   before they mate
a cicada   deposits her eggs   in slits cut into twigs

the body armor
discarded around the tree.

My father thought war   sounded like a high-pitched cicada   sex-fest
a cyclical   dis-assemblage
where the next brood   dug in

until a better time
on the surface.

[In his fever dream, uttering rapidly]

    Ghwó' shich' íí£é£*   my mother died   she left me
    (I was abandoned)   this is hurting me   dágóghé'áo**   naa£ni
                (I have difficulties) (illnesses)
They say   when we are ready
What we know   what we buried   what they slugged out of us
must   wake up. Be strong.

He says *must wake up*:   I think [awaken]
implying   to activate rouse stir liven energize get going.

    A story out-grown

    [means]   revived external to the frame   which muted us
        like cicada shells   peeled brittle membranes   clinging to limbs.

---
* Jicarilla to English, 454
** Ibid., 453

    We're done with what
    that story shelled   shelling us   bombarding us into shards
    local   hooligan   shenanigans
    slugging us purple   and baloney unleashed   on us
    as to who   is galavantin'
    on our lands   could be
    what's been killin' us 'til now.

The [blank] my father means to fill-in: pia[*] ama[**] mamá[***] máthair[****] mother.[*****]
Each narrator, Comanche, Basque, Spanish, Irish, English

peeled off   stripped down   his mother   tongue   shimaa[******]
[his root crisis] (linked to) [his mother's root crisis] I think he means
dispossession is removing and disassembling   children from mothers   mothers from kinship.

We painted this memory onto petrified slip-stone together   father and daughter.
    He felt this was the stump-fever people told him about.

A damp hand towel to his forehead
my fingers rest at his cheek
scarcely touching
to feel his struggled breathing.

---

[*] Comanche, mother, Comanche Vocabulary, Comanche-Spanish-English, Manuel García Rejón/Daniel J. Gelo.
[**] Basque, mother, www1.euskadi.net/morris/resultado.asp
[***] Spanish, mother, common usage.
[****] Irish-English, mother, common usage.
[*****] English, mom, common usage.
[******] Jicarilla Apache to English, mother, 326

On the move bending time [Enemy Slayer]

Dozens of flies think
they will escape
a twisted storm of wind.
The hairy one, a head like quivering desert weeds
foxtails in autumn
thinks he can possess

the contours of memory,   our story,   to the farthest glaciers
we know.
Thinks he'll replace the logographs
to convey creeks, leaves, and passages inside us.

Ndé* mizaa** nkaiyé***
is the "scroll" of land dreaming.

I emerged from love between thorns and rose
creating thunder, when wind pushed
forth the gray-light whirl.
I am a polity, the lawmaker, my grandmothers are
the roots of fecund rose and swan lady of the lake.
My father is hadntn pollen from where the universe begins.
I am in the first telling of Nigusdzán.

Shash shimaa hastin will tell me the next move, so I wait.
She says we can't hide   fear

if I walk away   the desecration
stench of cold moss and lime

                                I would be no more than grief
without heart   numb.

---

* Ndé Dene language

** Long walk; migration; deep-time presence

*** Earth is woman

A reluctant witness [Enemy Slayer]

This one came with a vengeance song.

Memories pour through him			like a sieve.

The star sang		ushered his dead across		and left.

A Killing field		a grow-out of blood-memory		seeding the soil.

She warned their life is like dust		feathers		pearls.

Faint shadows		spittle bone fractures		emptied bowels		drying blood
remaining		disfigured		dismembered.

Redress			is my compass.

Star People

Earth changes.

Change then remembrance.   Everything becomes fast
too lush   we awake and sleep   all dream.

Driving maps   petrified paintings   rock-art logograms
we downed   an agate   glittering mica   bent time

land hitting
dirt leaves vines   a place you were born.

Giving words to us   everything,   everything with weight
Horse   took   your   leg   &   gave you sight.

Witness   see the star
this world sends   another fire.

Off-the-record   occupation   is possessive and rules.
Possesses this realm   leap

you can't return.   Rather, you recycle through dimensions.

Star woman   escorts all   the abject
glittering world

mangled and coiled
under stars
                         Luna luna   your story to tell.

TIME | BENDING

[A]boriginal peoples did not vanish and are not stuck in the past.

[A]boriginal peoples are constantly made to feel as if they are
no longer as good as the imaginary "Indian" of the colonial imagination.

—Wanda Nanibush[17]

| Message to my father   who went to live
                                           with the End of the World People*

Your unanswered letters spiral about me.
My responses   left unsent.
You passed before I went to the post.

An urge gnaws
giving in to grief. You've gone. I couldn't

tell you about my two unborn fetus' death   chemical disasters in the desert
contamination in our blood.   Burying their curdled bodies.

I lied to you, lie continually about
how death makes me

deny my hate   of the space   you don't fill   and

disavow   the space   your death   demands   be filled.

---

* A phrase used by Dene peoples to denote Dene ancestors in the White Glittering world in the fourth position of the metaphysics of Dene time.

You were a universe being born

        Geodes bursting forth
        with vital messages for next life. I can't show you

        my daughters, the new child growing in my belly   her powerful thinking
head
        against the bone-ridge of cervix.

        The certainty that she's soaked in the DDT
        fused in our floorboards, soil, blood,
        the cellular swelling and membrane
        porosity inducing mutation.

        This is me, the possible link to the new you,
        the corpse, your vessel, decomposing; your free spirit cycling, refusing further debate.

        I loved you. Many times I hated the world hating you.
        Hated your fear of a hateful world   and how it corrodes your heart.
        Corroded.   Corroded heart

        of an Indian man who decided being Indian
        is what must be left behind. Everything buried

        is what you expect me to mine: stories unraveled in my dreams,
        your mother's mangled womb, your repentance,
blame
        confessed to priests, drunks, and strangers.

        I want to be mesquite bark, knotted,
        fused by selective memory. Ironwood in blossom, birthing fetuses
live
        and become children

        letting   down   letting the blood down
        placenta of our beginnings.

Loss tightens her hands around my larynx

I'm a waxy husk, hard June corn.

Loss etches   a line in my memory
the trap-line between   birth   Ndé Bizaa*   peeled

my tongue   barked
                                  hulled
                                  stripped
                                  pared

at age four   confessionals
at age seven   marching in line at East Terrell Hills
age eight   jumped by three White boys
age nine   chasing them down and beating one bloody
age ten   retaliations ensnaring more vengeance.

I smell   the boys'   sweat   on   his   nape
as   I chase   him   down; grab   his scalp hair,
shove   his   face   into   the   dirt.   His hot sweat
seeping   through   his white   t-shirt   wetting   my palms.

I remember
this.   When I   clearly knew

this *thing*   I   was becoming

was   *American.*

---

*My language

A lightning bolt   I see up ahead

    I put Texas in the rear-view   for good

    then   for good   again

    then   for good   for the last time

    then   finally

for   the good.

Dáyáada baa' ínjúúli | Native superstition

        In reality, mental constriction is compulsory.
        Texas is an open-air detention-hall.

Indigenous bodies and the settler poor
        managed   to being nothing   more than menial things: batteries.

        Things   sourced and   purposed.
Fabricated
        and tasked.

        When I left, I took I-10, Ft. Stockton to Redford   Uncle said
        we are
"unrecognized."   He said, "Our condition
        in Texas   is a silo.   Texas
        is a   storage   structure."

        Monsoon, colossal
        proportions.   I can't convey to you   its power
        Ndé
bodies   minds   our [feed storage] existence
        thingified
        Indians disavowed.   It seemed best to
        reduce risk, get ahead of a cataclysm.

        Cutting through Alberta, there are
distorted accounts   [sequential rationale]. We see
        nativists take nearest exit | to re-attest their beliefs. Worshipping
        centers   roadside   mytho-history markers   re-confirms

        Head smashed in   buffalo jump.
        Cracked skulls. Fractured limbs. Frenzy.

        Uncle says   "They write the story they crave."

Hypocrites and the Monster Slayer

      On the hard-pan

surface   the witless, frauds   divisive stories
      duplicitous [Native American]   storytellers   peddling turquoise
      etched silver   poet-tourists   haggling with worshippers
      taking the check

      reciting chapters, speeches, blogs, platforms

      pine, spruce, fir, and hemlock   pulped   into lyric verse, narrative, dramatic monologue.

      Clouds lapse   leaving only
      imperfect shores exposed by a low tide.

      A tentative creature
emerges   skitters
      miniscule   punctures   in sand.

      Nanasgané   [monster slayer]   roused

      sits up   feeling hungry   and exposed.

Baby graves   dágóyé'éé (it is difficult)*

Letters, reports, rumoring
legitimate indigenous histories   can't be written by the politically "dead."
Digital hearsay   posts   don't daunt me.

You didn't want to talk about the past, until now   in dreams.
Still you recorded a message about forgiveness
into a cassette   for the parish priest.

I buried a miscarried fetus
in a chasm made of
sink holes

deserted by mega-projects
fracking the land of memories.

Death remakes us
as invention.   Our struggle
to belong in place   beyond   shadow
          is our tyranny.

Our voices rebutting   state death
stirs the want   for our silence.

On our last phone call, you said
"Weaponizing Mexico will lead to mass killings
and this pushes refugees to our lands. We'll be pushed under, again."

---
* English to Jicarilla Apache, 453.

Dágóghé 'é (hard time)[*]

When my father's heart burst   a universe was born
quickening passage to [Dene end-of-life place].

Ndé don't die   the same as ndá.[**]

We are returned   to ancestors and rewoven onto spooled threads
as   eternal glittering colors   rewoven into precise places
made whole again   our tools made from star dust

to cut down the skeleton frame
of a toxic gokal (formerly: tipi) [now: house]
        to remove lead-mercury fillings

We return to recycled post-nuclear loosely familiar kinship
re-positioned in toxic soils
pulsing through our bloodstream.

Dad, Ndé rebirth   is
a possible
new heart-song for
an Indian man who decides
being dead   [to those who insist Lipans must play dead]
                              [and stay dead]
                              [to justify   the order of things]
is an idea you must molt
and shed.

---

[*] English to Jicarilla Apache, 451.
[**] White people

Dá 'aandí 'aa'*   (it is up to you)   April 15, 2018

I carry your cassette with me every time I travel by land or air. Today, while
flag-poling to update my NAFTA work permit, I secure your tape
in a tote. It nested snugly amongst office supplies picked up at Wal-Mart.
It's in the car trunk, as I approach the Aldergrove BC border crossing.
I have your last words bundled in a purple bandana I got in the craft aisle,
all 30% off.

Your last message

with me in passage.

What's your business in Canada?

                       I work and live here with my husband and children.

---

* English-to-Jicarilla, 453.

When the officer goes into his security kiosk and proceeds to review my FBI and CIC record
I presume the lengthy delay is due to being put on the national domestic watch list
after my mother counter-sued Michael Chertoff, the US Army and
the US Customs Border Patrol in 2008.

Who is your employer, and what is your line of work?

> *UBC Okanagan in the Syilx unceded territory.*
> *I am in the faculty of Indigenous Studies.*

When the officer returns to his computer and reviews the data bank, I presume his delay is related to factors on my record which underpin his next question.

And what do you research?

> *Poetry of dissidence; Indigenous peoples divided by nation-states and borders; militarization; Indigenous rights; Indigenous women's historical perspectives.*

I lied when I told the Queen's officer
I'm not carrying seeds, contraband
and have no large currency
nor undeclared weapons.

I am a seed, my research is deemed a threat to the US state, my knowledge is currency, and I am considered a weaponized threat of knowing, challenging normative Texas history and memory.

Do eighteen-foot gulag cement and steel walls   contain?

Checkpoint Charlie, drones, and razor wire
I've felt and known in Texas, Arizona, and Washington
count when I remember them
now   and   here? [I was thinking].

When the officer returns my passport
his knuckles shove my left shoulder and his fingers
grasp my shoulder tightly
for just a moment.

Did my face flinch
when the biometric cameras
flashed in my direction?

Do the shoves   of the wall
register on my body's   conditioned and rehearsed   stillness
under interrogation?

Post-survivor

Earth
her veined web-shield

now broken
her roots now dying

fragile universe
now mined

excavated stories
lipping off

nightmares, ghouls
skin walkers

assailing

the root canal of time
disgracing ozone-thin membranes of light

birthing—the untired—
pitching headfirst

unscathed
emerging power-hungry.

WHAT'S COMING

Under the crease of sky

My father can't be told *I can't stay*   my hands push
the enclosing.

At the edge of his new arrangement
I meet him in the traveling place.

I'm the grieving daughter   in-between
creases where dead disappear someplace everywhere anyplace.

His hands cross space: blue-veined   papery skin; smooth, clean nails.
Had to be clean   ought required driven compelled ordered
to be clean.
Oblate Mary Immaculata commandeered his head.

In dreams, he tells me to make prayers, visit relatives.
Doors shut, re-opened   here in   another "Indian
Country"   through bordered disorder.

At death, he lifted.   I wanted to stay and see (realize, perceive, grasp)
then afraid I might never get back   (drift, stay)

To liquid flow   time without fear.
Time bending.

Bending | the word | with my father

Though you died in '96, I bring your words back from dreams.
Right after hearing your words, I want them.

They are difficult to manage.
I need them to land

onto my palm, be brought back to time
in flux.

They came from someone in the dream
reading about string theory

and pulling gold-tipped illustrated words
from an accordion.
The player's fingers summon one sound
at a time

reminding me of long memory
between exaggeration and effort
and in dream you said I should save one word
in a napkin
for later

because you minded as our other words began slipping out of their skins
like over-ripe plums, all veiny. You (re)minded me to
soothe words from leaving my memory, and you said

all I had to do was to lick and taste them into long memory.
Some words passed through clouded spaces between my fingers
and with each disappearance   the land rumbled
there were so many ways words and memory and feeling could disappear.

The word meant everything
in the dream.

In dreams, the suspension of memory
is a lucid fact.

Your words' fingers held mine and
I remembered your death.

Our memories met briefly inside a circle of words, when suddenly the dream ended.

At the entombment

A month after his funeral, in dream #32, [December, 1996]
my father meets me at a path

he sits on top of a headstone and shapes himself
into "footnote 1."
As an annotated footer, he recalls the names
of many converted and hidden Dene Ndé			that is, unaccounted for Lipan Apaches
still traveling across the Alaska-Yukon		Texas-Mexico		cuts	and	divisions

and, who live death in state. He points: "this very spot" where they
came into history as Catholicized tombstone names: Maria, José, Jesus, Mary, Joseph.

My father's mouth opens and orates (by memory)
the refusal of spirit		abduction and punishment.

Even at the site of the massacre		he refuses political death.

In this queue, [time |||| bending] Dene Ndé die incrementally			in a spectrum
by edicts, acts, policies,
procedures, motions, pleas,
commissions, flags, conspiracies,
death marches, dungeons, lynchings,
round-ups, cattle car train-transfers, gulags,
walls, drones, stadium lights, surveillance, state stalking,
clandestine dirty wars, JTF6 normalized,
duplicity. Necro politics

has no

past participle present future imperfect.

My father stays earthbound

You resist going   though you don't know why you can't   go on.
Halfling. Half-way. Not there not here.   Everywhere.

Dead and half-living.   Still, a color wheel orbs you.
You prove a binary is place   where lies begin.

I don't think I should call you "dead" or "dad."

These experiences I call "dream"
entwine me in fields.

This time   you stand in a forest   bears at the fringe
                                    scrutinize   sniff air   go on.

You say you're done   with those who hate   as a form
of nothing else to do.

You ask   if I am loving   what I will become
when I wake up.

Night will color a dream real different

In dream #17, I take to air on the back of an alloyed resolve   to tell you
stop showing up.

In lucid dream #24, I assemble wings   muscular and wide   to hurry
me to the bending place.

There you are standing with Shashisdzan* hastiin**   and your Inuit friend
in Suline ko'.***

Down to a lower world   I bend   to meet you.

---

*NWT Dene MacKenzie River country; ancestral Dene Ndé homelands before the 2nd migration (15,000 BC)

**chiefly person

***NWT Dene MacKenzie River country; ancestral Dene Ndé homelands before the 2nd migration (15,000 BC)

Dream #27 Gowá shimaa [my mother's house]

My mourning shimaa* kneels on a pew;
through her black veil is her distorted profile   her face constricts

She cries   like other Indians I know, who spin the modern
oral tradition from daily grief   a spinning roulette.

In her gowá**
grief is the seducer.
Without a weapon or a mask she didn't get
what he was about.
This is her house. A house of water.

Crying is lacrimation   lagrimas   la cremation   though
he didn't burn.

Some menopausal aunts stand in prayer with new babies
they've birthed.
I don't question it; dreams being that way.   Elder women birth babies
in travel bending.

---

* mother
** home, house, dwelling; motherplace

Father replays the funeral in Dream #28

Shame   forces   what we denied   into luminosity.
In dream   my father   tells me   my mother's grieving
prevents   momentum.

He's projecting thoughts onto a screen   for me to read.
I'm at his private film   of captivity.

He's watching us.   We're hunched over   heaving the sorrow vomit.

Father stands before me
time without fear   suspended   and apart
unafraid of anything   one way or another.

"When did they cut it?"   he wants to know   pushing the thought
into space   between my eyes.

Raising his pant leg   where the mortician

smoothed and stretched the salvage skin   Father used   for padding
his below-knee amputation
hovering   inches above the ground   glints in his eyes.

He doesn't remember the amputation
in the bending.

Father shows me his whole leg.   Scars

mended and smooth.
He is an uncut body again. Like before the bending place.
Only the graft scars on his thighs remain.

He projects: "I feel my leg *here*   Margo   my foot still itches *here*"   Father points:
"in this empty space"   he twirls his fingers   a   slow   spiral.

I nod to him and project to the screen: "I see. I'll remember this."

My father's nickname tł'éna 'áí si'a | moonlight   luna

Fill in this vast space   between you and what you've done to yourself.

Elegant, muscular hands   massaged away the bombs
making us shrapnel.   Your easy women, mother figures, users.

I wanted skin as dark as his   the seal   the otter   the little beauty:
precious Luna, Luna   the glowlight

Running back Luna
Cross-country Luna
Marathon Luna
Four-year   letterman   Luna

Baby baby Luna
moon and glow
is what held you together.

What's coming

In bendingtimeplace   my father doesn't remember his death.

Watching me   with

big Betty Boop "ooh-ooh-ooh-ooh"   eyes   and I feel he's doing that on purpose.
He disbelieves the flux   is anything more than architecture.

Disbelieves   he and I are suspended
in the bendingtimeplace.

He's wondering   and asks   "when can we get ice cream"
                                                for waiting this out

for following sequences of events
inside the lineage weaving family and colonial history

for the required false pledge to our oppressors
all the while masking dissent   as we vision their karmic necrosis

bringing us   to the root reason
my father is somewhat somewhere   here-there   sticking   stuck

on the side of the   Dene-in-limbo   routing to   Dene-in-migration
who reach   the abalone   returning whirlwind cave-entrance

but remain   stuck-stuck   living and dead.

140

What's still coming

"I want to tell you something   about
what's coming"
Ooh-ooh   blink-blink.

His smile rising at the corners of his laughter,

chortling from   yummy vanilla caramel

in frozen droplets   at the corners of his mouth.

"But I'm not allowed to"   Ooh-ooh   Blink.

Very   oracular of him.

Just   as in life
at the very moment   I begin to hear   and feel him
he vanishes.

My father wants a ceremony because the funeral wasn't helpful   1996

He left a message.

I remind myself, when I awake, sheets and blankets coiled
like vipers, I can barely move to sit up
sweat trickles along my breasts, curves around my calves. I'm irritated.

He wants a ceremony, he wants a *gathering*
a circle of women huddled around a table
holding his body;
he instructs me.

He's wearing the lilac-colored shirt, a favorite from the '70s.
Paler, his eyes contact, not gazing to the side   of former dreams

no longer the flirt   there is no time.

When he moves around the table, hovering
he takes me to a place where time isn't slurred by fear.

He says, "This is necessary.

What I come back to

is not necessarily everything."

I get lost *twice*, following him.
He finds me and says
"The way out is the *only* way in."

Dream: He re-emplaces to a gokal nadekleshen nigusdzaan*

My father is not human
but form; more than the word
he is the word with a body.

The body of the father he was
is under a shade structure in the desert
not heaven   sacred   in another way, and palm fronds shelter the gathering people.

I'm worried.   I want to wake up.
I don't want to know more.

Flicker-glitter-listener.
I am.
He pushes this thought.

His hair is black and long to the hips
"Be here   calm   sit now   listen

and we (relatives)   all in sections   (of time)
with earth

We are no longer with people   [we knew]   on earth.
We are no longer people."

There is an order   my former-father
now-spirit   knows.

How is it to be? I ask him.

"Good."

"Not to be touched   I am."

Glittery   stillness   time opening.

---

* The house of Earth-is-Woman's god-mothers.

WALLED IN

Walled in by history, we stay alive, we remain, nonetheless

Denying genocide in Kónitsąąíígokíyaa   holsters
distorted history,   an American gun.

Revisionist denial   blames   beautiful us,
our indigeneity,   for being a messy, bloody   dis-order.

Trolling   our indigeneity   as   un-fit
     memory   memorywork   story.   The ledgers hidden.

Ledgers   we embody.   A wind tunnel of
#ndn #authenticity   #blood #hunting   throwing down #destructive #impulses.

Denial   a #final stage   though   denying   implies perpetual motion
our embodied   exist   stance   has no exit   #inthistrap #strap.

Neocolonial   double kill.
Collective numbing   begets collective   denial.   Curious:

Did your hands   choke out   my   mouth full   of
front line   rage?   Did your   fingers   force death

as deletion   on our   lacunaed   unrecognized   exist   stance?
Do you swipe left   or right   when we   show up   unexpectedly?

How do you   show up?   Do you strive   for what I need to commemorate?
Do you tone   and tune   #out   my recovery?   My reassembling?

Do you stalk   me   for   pulling together   my family's fragments,
our shatter zones   of the crime?

Did you   feel   unsettled   that my   sight line   is an   earthline
      walled in,   exiled   inside   carceral

Indigenous herstory rising?   That I'm uncoiled   bitten   scarred   drenched in
memory's bright sun   in desolation's   exhausted   moon. I'm

       blueorangepurpleyellowredbrownblackgreenochre
knowing   differently,   we remained   we stay alive

none   the   less.

Notes

[1] Patrick Wolfe, "Settler Colonialism and the Elimination of the Native," *Journal of Genocide Research*.

[2] Ndé symbol of Ndé belonging and Native sovereignty in Kónítsaįįgokĺyąą, Big Water Country (Rio Grande River water world).

[3] Thomas Brudholm and Valérie Rosoux, "The Unforgiving: Reflections on the Resistance to Forgiveness after Atrocity," *Law and Contemporary Problems*, Vol. 72, No. 2, Group-Conflict Resolution: Sources of Resistance to Reconciliation (Spring 2009), pp. 33-49: 38.

[4] After Carter, Rodney GS. "Of things said and unsaid: Power, archival silences, and power in silence." *Archivaria* 61 (2006): 215-233.

[5] Ibid.

[6] George Blondin, *Yamoria the Lawmaker: Stories of the Dene*. NeWest Press, 1997: 82-84.

[7] Darryl Coote. Texas dioceses publish some 300 names of clergy accused of sexually abusing minors." United Press International. https://www.upi.com/Top_News/US/2019/01/31/Texas-dioceses-publish-some-300-names-of-clergy-accused-of-sexually-abusing-minors/4191548993468/. Accessed June 26, 2020.

[8] A. McCormack, M D Janus, A W Burgess. "Ruanaway Youths and Sexual Victimizaation: Gender Differences in an Adolescent Runaway Population." *Child Abuse & Neglect*. 1986;10(3):387-395. doi:10.1016/0145-2134(86)90014-1

[9] Ben Kiernan. *Blood and Soil: A World History of Genocide and Extermination from Sparta to Darfur*. New Haven: Yale University Press, 2007, 335; See also, Tamez, Margo. "NÁDASI 'NÉ 'NDÉ'ISDZÁNÉ BEGOZ'AAHÍ'SHIMAA SHINÍ'GOKAL GOWĄ GOSHJAA HA 'ÁNÁ 'IDŁÍ TEXAS-NAKAIYÉ GODESDZOG Translation." PhD diss., Washington State University, 2010.

[10] Harry Hoijer, "The History and Customs of the Lipan, As Told by Augustina Zuazua." Linguistics. 161: 5-38. 1975.

[11] Handbook of Texas Online, John R. Ross, "LYNCHING," accessed June 30, 2020, http://www.tshaonline.org/handbook/online/articles/jgl01.

[12] David Frye, *Indians into Mexicans: History and Identity in a Mexican Town*, Austin: University of Texas Press, 1996: 4.

[13] Kirby Brown, "Historical Recovery, Colonial Mimicry, and Thoughts on Disappearing Indians in Elena Zamora O'Shea's El Mesquite." Retrieved from http://indigenouscultures.org/blog

[14] Dustin Tahmahkera, "Hakarʉ Marʉʉmatʉ Kwitaka? Seeking Representational Jurisdiction in Comanchería Cinema," *Native American and Indigenous Studies*, Vol. 5, No. 1 (Spring 2018), pp. 100-135, University of Minnesota Press. Stable URL: https://www.jstor.org/stable/10.5749/natiindistudj.5.1.0100

[15] Reviel Netz, *Barbed Wire: An Ecology of Modernity*, Middleton: Wesleyan University Press, 2004: 53.

[16] Ibid., 49.

[17] Wanda Nanibush, "The Frozen Bodies of Edward S. Curtis," Review, *Literary Review of Canada*, April 4, 2011: 4-5.

About the Author

Margo Tamez is a poet, herstorian, activist, and Indigenous feminist critic. Her previous publications include *Raven Eye* (The University of Arizona Press 2007), *Naked Wanting* (The University of Arizona Press 2003), and a chapbook, *Alleys & Allies* (Saddle Tramp Press 1991). She holds a B.A. in Archaeological Studies (1984), a B.A. in Art History (1985), University of Texas at Austin, an M.F.A. in Poetry (1997) from the Creative Writing Program at Arizona State University, and a PhD in American Studies [Emphasis: Critical Lipan women's history].

She is the recipient of regional and national awards, though counts her most significant award the Poetry Fellowship from the Arizona Commission on the Arts in 1999, in early years of her writing career, which made it possible to pay the balance on her three-acre parcel in Akimel O'odham traditional territory and to re-think her future as a poet, writer, and herstorian. Her work has appeared in critical sites, such as *American Poetry Review*, *Cimarron Review*, *Hawaii Pacific Review*, *Missouri Review*, among others, and her work has achieved national and international recognition in critical collections such as *Indigenous Message on Water* (United Nations World Forum on Water, 2015), *Entre Guadalupe y Malinche: Tejanas in Literature and Art* (University of Texas Press, 2015), and *Dance the Guns to Silence: 100 Poems for Ken Saro-Wiwa* (2005). Tamez is an internationally recognized author, criss-crossing boundaries, and embodying the advancement of Indigenous poetics. Her writing on Indigenous memory and witness, in poetry, criticism, international law, and justice, is extensive. Her work on critical revitalization of Ndé knowledge and language underscores the resurgence of Ndé self-determination and control over Ndé knowledge, being, and belonging.

She is an enrolled citizen of the Lipan Apache Band, Texas, and born to original of Kónitsąąíígokíyaa'en descendants and relative to the Gochish (Lightning), Cuélcah'én (Tall Grass, 'Prairie' or 'Plains'), and Shash (Bear) lineal societies, which includes relative Jumano Apache, Comanche Apache, Kiowa Apache, Nahua Apache, and Tlaxcalteca Apache peoples. She is the third daughter of Eloisa Garcia Tamez and Luis Carrasco Tamez, who shared and taught the extended kinship ties to sacred sites; ceremonial, Indigenous, and traditional medicinal systems; and river-based governance systems throughout Kónitsąąíígokíyaa beyond borders.

Margo Tamez is currently an associate professor in the faculty of Indigenous Studies at the University of British Columbia | Okanagan, and lives on Sqilxw land at N'sis'ooloxw, BC, Canada. She divides her time between El Calaboz, N'sis'ooloxw Nk'mlpqs, Dene sites of significance (beyond borders), and the timebendingfluxplace.

www.ingramcontent.com/pod-product-compliance
Lightning Source LLC
Chambersburg PA
CBHW051607170426
43196CB00040B/2972